Jackie Jones has worked at Edinburgh University Press for many years. In addition to her publishing career, she has undertaken numerous vegan cookery, restaurant-level courses and masterclasses in the UK, and has a Vegan Diploma and Advanced Vegan Diploma from Demuths Cookery School, Bath.

THE SCOTTISH VEGAN COOKBOOK

Plant-Based Recipes for Everyday Eating

Jackie Jones

BIRLINN

A BIG VEGAN SHOUT OUT

A vegan revolution is taking place in Scotland. In cities and towns across the country, local cafés, restaurants, market stalls and food festivals are offering an ever growing set of options for vegan diners, and some are completely vegan. Not all provide traditionally Scottish food, so if you want to veganise some of your favourite Scottish dishes at home this is the book for you.

The recipes in *The Scottish Vegan Cookbook* show you how to prepare a wide variety of tasty plant-based dishes drawing on Scotland's abundant seasonal vegetables, fruits and whole grains. There are recipes for well-known favourites such as Cullen skink, haggis, 'neeps and tatties', Scotch broth, clootie dumpling and cranachan. I've added a modern twist to old recipes such as orange and carrot 'posset', healthy salads and soups using Scottish ingredients, and some contemporary updates, such as Scotch mist, using meringues made with aquafaba.

The long tradition of Scottish cookery incorporates the culinary influences of other cuisines, and there are many international and fusion dishes which make up the current cookery and restaurant scene. While I have drawn on techniques and ingredients from other countries (such as French-inspired sauces or Asian miso and tofu), I have focused on offering vegan versions of culturally identifiable Scottish 'classics'.

Throughout the book I have aimed to take into account current thinking about what constitutes a nutritionally balanced vegan diet. I have often used alternatives to refined white sugar, bleached white flour and industrially processed fats, although there is still a place for some indulgent puddings and desserts!

The following recipes use ingredients that most people can find at their local farmers' market or in greengrocers, health-food shops or supermarkets without the need to source exotic or uncommon items further afield. The recipes are not complicated, although one or two use quite a long list of ingredients. Don't be daunted – these are often herbs or condiments to build up the flavour profile of a dish and they can be set out in advance.

There are recipes here for brunches, soups and breads, salads, main courses, vegetable accompaniments and desserts, as well as plant-based 'basics' such as oat milk, vegan butter, cream, custard, ice cream and tomato ketchup. Whether you are a novice cook looking for guidance, a keen cook looking to expand your repertoire or a professional chef looking to add Scottish vegan options to your menu, I hope you enjoy trying out some of these recipes.

CONTENTS

A VEGAN DIET

A well-balanced vegan or plant-based diet needs to include a wide variety of macronutrients – fat, carbohydrates and protein – together with essential micronutrients – vitamins, minerals and trace minerals. The staples for a healthy vegan diet are starchy foods such as whole grains (which keep the grain intact, including the germ and the bran) together with fruit, healthy fats (more about this follows), nuts, pulses, vegetables, seeds and soya-based foods.

I offer some common sense indicators here about the nutritional needs of vegans according to current nutritional thinking. I have concentrated on some of the key areas where vegans need to be sure they are eating sufficient plant-derived nutrients or are supplementing them adequately. This information is based on reading a range of books on vegan nutrition, on recommendations from vegan organisations such as Viva! and the Vegan Society, on UK and US government health websites and on the nutrition modules that I took for my vegan cookery diplomas. The information has also been checked by a qualified vegan nutritional therapist. If you have concerns about your nutritional needs, however, do consult your general health practitioner or a nutritional therapist who can work with you on your specific nutritional requirements.

PROTEIN

Advice about protein in vegan diets from advisory groups such as Viva! is that you can get enough protein by eating a healthy and varied nutrient-rich and whole-food vegan diet.

The science bit in brief: of the at least 20 different amino acids that can form a protein in the body there are nine which

A word about . . . quinoa

Quinoa currently has the status of being something of a wonder food. While it has been grown for thousands of years by the Incas high up in the Andes, it is now grown in Britain! Hodmedod's are the main supplier of British-grown quinoa, as well as other pulses and grains. Quinoa can be found in supermarkets and in health food shops.

As well as containing protein, quinoa is full of dietary fibre, iron, magnesium, manganese and phosphorus. It is also gluten-free and easy to digest. Rinse it thoroughly before use to remove the bitter coating around the grain.

the body cannot produce by itself, known as 'Essential' Amino Acids (EAAs). These must be obtained from our diet. In order to be a 'complete' protein, foods must contain all nine EAAs in about equal proportions.

Some plant-based foods *are* 'complete' proteins. According to the NutritionData website (nutritiondata.self.com/), these include amaranth, buckwheat, chia seeds, hemp seeds, quinoa, seitan (pronounced 'say-tan', which is made with vital wheat gluten flour), soya beans and spirulina.

Getting enough protein should not be difficult for vegans if we eat a wide array of plant-based proteins. While our protein requirements vary, the NHS recommends an intake of 55g per day for men and 45g for women.

Most plant foods contain the nine EAAs needed to build protein in our bodies, just not always individually in the ideal proportions. However, current nutritional thinking is that we do not need to consume all of our EAAs in one go, or even every day. Therefore we can meet our protein needs by eating from a wide variety of food groups, including:

- Beans: such as black beans, chickpeas, fava beans, kidney beans and peanuts, the higher protein options being black beans (around 21g per 100g), chickpeas (around 19g per 100g) and peanuts, which are a legume (around 25g per 100g serving).
- Nutritional Yeast: a very high source of plant protein at around 40g per 100g; a single serving is about a tablespoon of nutritional yeast flakes.
- Nuts: such as almonds, cashews and pistachios, with almonds packing in 21g of protein per 100g, with a serving being around 30g.
- Pulses: such as lentils, which provide around 9g per 100g, with 150g being an average serving.
- Seeds: such as pumpkin seeds, sesame seeds and sunflower seeds, as well as amaranth, buckwheat, chia seeds and hulled hemp seeds, each containing around 18g of protein per 100g, with 30g being a serving.
- Soya-based foods: including soya beans and edamame beans (young soya beans), soya milk, tempeh and tofu, with tempeh providing 18g of protein per 100g compared with tofu at around 8g per 100g.
- Spirulina: derived from seaweed and a source of plentiful protein (as well as of calcium and magnesium), providing around 57g of protein per 100g. Although expensive, a serving is just a teaspoonful.
- Vegetables: such as broccoli, garden peas, mushrooms and spinach.
- Whole Grains: such as brown rice, bulgur wheat and whole oats.

Easy ways to pick up protein are by eating baked potatoes with hummus; baked beans on toast; peanut butter wholemeal sandwiches; brown rice and beans; soya yoghurt with sunflower seeds or nut butter; scrambled tofu; wholewheat spaghetti and tomato sauce made with rapeseed oil and almonds; and eating amaranth, buckwheat or quinoa instead of white rice and pasta.

You can also supplement protein intake with protein powders such as pea protein and hemp protein, which you can add to breakfast bowls, soups, smoothies, biscuits and cakes.

Tryptophan

Tryptophan is an essential amino acid which helps with general growth and development and is converted in the body to serotonin – known as the mood enhancer.

Plant foods rich in tryptophan include almonds, beans, buckwheat, cashew nuts, chia seeds, flax seeds, garden peas, lentils, millet, oats, pistachio nuts, pumpkin seeds, sesame seeds, spinach, spirulina, tofu, watermelon seeds and wheat germ.

VITAMINS AND MINERALS

Vitamin B12

B12 is required for a healthy nervous system, to prevent anaemia, for a healthy heart and circulation and for our uptake of protein. I have started this section with B12 because this is a vital vitamin which needs to be supplemented for vegans – and arguably for non-vegans as well – because it is not reliably available from plant sources or in sufficient amounts from other food.

Some breakfast cereals, nutritional yeast flakes, plant milks, soya-based foods, vegan butters, vegan stock powders, yeast extract/Marmite and plain vegan yoghurts are fortified with B12 (i.e. the vitamin is added to them). Of these, the best sources, according to Viva!, per average portion are fortified yeast extract (enough to spread on one slice of toast) and fortified soya milk (a glass of around 200ml).

The Vegan Society currently recommends either eating foods fortified with vitamin B12 two or three times a day *or* taking a B12 supplement daily of at least 10 micrograms *or* taking a B12 supplement weekly of at least 2,000 micrograms. If taking a supplement, it is still possible to eat foods fortified with B12 as well.

For further information see the websites of the Vegan Society or Viva! Heath.

Supplements are available in tablet and chewable tablet form or as a liquid supplement that can be taken sub-lingually (i.e. dissolved under the tongue).

Vitamin A

Although Vitamin A is only available from animals, our bodies are able to convert beta-carotene into the vitamin, which is required for growth, heart health, a well-functioning immune system, and healthy skin and vision. Foods rich in beta-carotene are predominantly orange, red and yellow fruit and vegetables, although don't overlook green veg! Good sources include:

butternut squash, cantaloupe melon, carrots and carrot juice, dried apricots, mango, papaya, peaches, peppers, pumpkin and sweet potatoes, as well as broccoli, chard, kale, spinach, tomatoes (cooked) and watercress.

- *Vitamins A, D, K and E are fat-soluble vitamins, and so best eaten with a little healthy fat.*

Vitamin B2 (Riboflavin)
Vitamin B2 is required for energy, healthy hair, nails and skin. Useful sources include almonds, avocados, broccoli, cabbage, dark green leafy vegetables, dried prunes, mushrooms, pumpkin, soya-based foods, tomatoes, watercress, wheat germ and yeast extract.

Vitamin C
Vitamin C is essential for the body's tissue growth and repair, for the body's absorption of iron and for healthy teeth, bones and skin, and its antioxidant qualities help to boost the immune system. Vegans who eat a wide range of fruits and vegetables should be sufficient in vitamin C. Excellent plant-based sources include: bell peppers, blackcurrants, blueberries, broccoli, Brussels sprouts, cantaloupe melon, cauliflower, garden peas, grapefruit, kale, kiwi fruit, lemons, mango, oranges, papaya, pineapple, potatoes, raspberries, spinach (fresh), spring greens, strawberries and tomatoes. You can get your daily amount from eating just one orange, a handful of strawberries, or three or four florets of cooked broccoli.

Calcium and Vitamin D
Calcium is needed for healthy bones and teeth (although other vitamins and minerals play a part in bone health, besides calcium). It also helps to regulate our heartbeat and other muscle contractions, sustains our nervous systems and plays a vital role in blood clotting.

Plant-based sources of calcium include aduki beans, almonds and fortified almond milk, almond butter, amaranth, artichokes, avocados, baked beans, black beans, blackcurrants, black-eyed beans, blackberries, blackstrap molasses, bok choy, brazil nuts, broccoli, cabbage, cannellini beans, chia seeds, chickpeas, dates, dried apricots (if you can, buy the unsulphured variety which are dark in colour), dried figs, fennel (raw), haricot beans (navy beans), hemp milk, hummus, kale, kidney beans, lentils, mustard greens, okra, oranges and orange juice, parsley, peas, quinoa, raisins, seaweed, sesame seeds and tahini, soya beans and other soya products (such as fortified soya milk, calcium-set tofu, soya yoghurt and tempeh), spring greens (collard greens), sweet potato, turnip greens and watercress.

The most 'bioavailable' – that is, the most easily absorbable – calcium-rich plant-based foods include broccoli, calcium-enriched tofu, cauliflower,

A word about . . . tofu

Tofu, or soya bean curd, is a very good source of calcium, the more so if it is firm and set with calcium sulfate (gypsum), such as the Taifun brand, and also – if a little less so – if it is silken or set with magnesium chloride (nigari). Smoked and herb-flavoured tofu are also now readily available. Using warm liquids helps tofu infuse flavours more effectively: try marinading cubes of tofu for 30 minutes or so in a saucepan of warm almond milk mixed with a teaspoon of vegan stock, a sprinkle of garlic granules, some fresh oregano and fresh thyme and a little black pepper. Add to soups and stews (with the liquid).

dried figs, fortified almond, rice and soya milk, fortified orange juice, kale, sesame seeds and tahini, spring greens (collard greens) and watercress. Nutritional experts Jack Norris and Virginia Messina suggest in their book *Vegan for Life* (p. 44; pp. 45–6 and p. 88) that it is best to obtain calcium from several different foods which are rich in the mineral, including a wide range of dark green leafy vegetables and soya products. They emphasise that frozen dark green leafy vegetables, because of their volume, actually have a higher amount of calcium than fresh.

Our calcium needs vary according to age and gender. Although different parts of the world seem to have different daily recommended minimum intakes, 700mg is the UK minimum for an adult, rising to 1,000mg for a male over the age of 50 and 1,300mg for a female over the age of 50.

If we aim for 1,000mg of calcium we need to eat around six to eight servings of calcium-rich foods every day. A serving is equal to around two tablespoons of almond butter, two figs, two oranges, 125g calcium-set tofu, 125ml of calcium-fortified fruit juice or 250g of cooked broccoli or kale.

Try the recipe for calcium-rich Super Salad (p. 108)!

As a means of meeting our daily calcium requirements there is also the option to include foods fortified with calcium such as fortified orange juice and fortified plant milks (such as almond and soya).

Blackstrap molasses is a particularly rich source of calcium, with two tablespoons providing around two-fifths of our daily calcium needs. Other good sources are spring greens (collard greens) and turnip greens.

In order to ensure there is enough calcium in the diet, try adding chopped dried figs and a sprinkle of sesame seeds to your breakfast cereal or raisins to your porridge made with calcium-fortified plant milk. Add a spoonful of blackstrap molasses to your cake batters or spread hummus on oatcakes for lunch or a snack.

- *Note that spinach, rhubarb, chard and beetroot greens reduce the absorption of calcium due to the presence of oxalic acid in these foods.*

Vitamin D

Vitamin D is needed for balancing the amount of calcium and phosphate contained in the body, for healthy bones and teeth, maintaining our immune systems, aiding skin health, contributing to the healthy functioning of the nervous system and influencing mood, memory and the recovery of our muscles.

While we can make vitamin D from being outside in summer sunlight and vegans have a plant-based source of the vitamin in mushrooms (especially dried shiitake and morel mushrooms), current thinking is that we should be supplementing with at least 400IU of vitamin D daily. In the UK it is possible to take a test supplied by the NHS (for a fee of c.£29) to determine your levels of vitamin D before deciding on the amount you should take.

We can also look to fortified tofu and plant milks for this vitamin. Note that vitamin D2 is always vegan but vitamin D3 – which our bodies absorb more readily – may not be. Look for D3 supplements derived from lichen, which are becoming increasingly easy to find.

Alongside vitamin D, we need magnesium and vitamin K in order to absorb calcium effectively (see below).

- *Mushrooms need to be cooked for their nutrients to be released (raw mushrooms contain some toxins). Fortunately, the vitamin D is not destroyed during cooking.*

Vitamin E

Vitamin E contributes to the health of our eyes and skin, as well as effective circulation and a strong immune system. Plant sources include almonds, avocado, broccoli, dark leafy greens, hazelnuts, olive oil, peanuts, pecan nuts, spinach, sunflower seeds, sweet potato, wheat germ and wholemeal bread.

Iodine

Iodine is essential for thyroid function and is required for metabolising food into the body's energy. It can be obtained from plant sources such as apple juice, bananas, dark-green leafy vegetables, garden peas, pears, prunes, spirulina and watercress, but in quite small amounts. Seaweed also contains iodine. Some, such as different varieties of kelp (arame, kombu and wakame), are very iodine-rich and should be consumed in very small amounts. Hijiki is best to avoid with respect to possible arsenic content.

The best source of iodine is iodised salt used in moderation – around a half teaspoon providing you with your daily needs. As table salt is more processed (involving extraction mining) than sea salt, you might want to opt for iodised sea salt if you are not taking a supplement that includes iodine (such as VEG 1 – see below).

Iron

Iron is required for producing red blood cells and for preventing anaemia. Adequate intake of iron can be achieved from a variety of plant-based sources if a little care is taken in the way in which they are prepared and eaten with other foods.

Plant-based sources of iron include: asparagus, baked potatoes, broccoli, Brussels sprouts, chickpeas, dried fruit, garden peas, kale, lentils, mushrooms (especially morel), nuts, oatmeal, oats, olives, parsley, prune juice, pulses, pumpkin and pumpkin seeds, quinoa, raisins, soya beans and soya-based foods including tempeh and tofu, sesame seeds, spinach (cooked), spirulina, sun-dried tomatoes, Swiss chard, tomato paste, watercress, wheat germ, white beans, whole grains and wholemeal bread and flour. Fortified foods include Marmite and yeast extract.

Morel mushrooms, cooked soya beans and sun-dried tomatoes are particularly good plant sources of iron.

Plant foods containing iron such as bran, grains, nuts and seeds, beans and other pulses also contain phytic acid, which prevents iron absorption unless these foods are heated, soaked, sprouted or fermented and combined with vitamin C-rich foods. Use vinegar in salad dressings to enhance mineral absorption and cook food in an iron pan to assist with iron absorption.

Some iron-rich vegetables such as spinach, broccoli, cabbage, chard and kale also contain iron-inhibiting oxalic acid and ideally need to be steamed (or boiled) and the water discarded.

In order to maximise iron intake at a meal, it is best to limit plant foods containing high levels of the polyphenols which inhibit iron absorption (which include black tea, coffee and cocoa). Also limit intake of calcium-rich plant foods with an iron-rich meal and take a calcium supplement or foods fortified with calcium separately.

For further information about iron uptake have a look at the Iron Disorders Institute website (www.irondisorders.org/diet/).

- *Iron is best absorbed when eaten with plant foods rich in vitamin C (and which do not contain too much calcium) such as bananas, grapefruit and grapefruit juice, pineapple and pineapple juice, bell peppers, cabbage, carrots, cauliflower, courgettes, cucumbers, mushrooms and full-size or canned tomatoes and tomato juice.*

Vitamin K

Vitamin K is needed for blood clotting, storing energy, a healthy liver and keeping our bones strong. There are two types of K vitamin – K1 and K2. K1 is found in dark-green leafy vegetables and some other vegetables. K2 can be found in fermented foods, including fermented cabbage. Natto – a traditional Japanese food made with fermented soya beans – is high in vitamin K2.

Good plant-based sources of vitamin K are alfalfa sprouts, artichoke hearts, asparagus, basil, beet greens, blackstrap molasses, bok choy, broccoli, Brussels sprouts, cabbage, carrots, cauliflower, chicory, green beans, kale, kiwi fruit, mustard greens, oregano, rocket, romaine lettuce, sage, soya beans, spinach, spring greens (collard greens), strawberries, swiss chard, thyme, turnip greens, watercress and whole grains, as well as olive oil and rapeseed oil.

The best source per 100g of food is kale, with one serving providing more than our daily needs, followed by spinach, broccoli, Brussels sprouts and cabbage.

Magnesium

Magnesium helps convert vitamin D into an active form, which our bodies further convert for calcium absorption. It also helps our muscles relax and can be useful for improving sleep. Our bodies use up magnesium very quickly when we're stressed. Plant-based sources include dark-green leafy vegetables, nuts and seeds.

Potassium

Potassium plays a part in controlling blood pressure, healthy cell function and nerves. Good foods include bananas, beans, blackstrap molasses, carrots and carrot juice, chard, dried fruit, garden peas, lentils, millet, brazil nuts, orange juice, potatoes, quinoa, raisins, root vegetables, sea vegetables, soya beans, spinach, sunflower seeds, sweet potatoes, tomatoes and wholemeal bread.

Selenium

Selenium contains antioxidants and plays an important role in healthy thyroid function and heart health. It can be found in avocados, brazil nuts, brown rice, bread, cashew nuts, chickpeas, lentils, mushrooms, potatoes, oatmeal, pasta, pecan nuts, pearl barley, seaweed, sesame seeds, sunflower seeds, walnuts, whole grains, wholemeal flour and yeast extract/Marmite.

A word about . . . fermentation and sprouting

By fermenting and sprouting foods, we can increase the availability of minerals to our bodies as well as making foods more digestible. Excellent sources of fermented foods for vegans include miso, tempeh and yeast-leavened bread. Soaking, then toasting nuts and seeds can help mineral absorption and gut health.

Many types of beans and grains can be sprouted (although not larger beans, as they may agitate the gut). Follow the method outlined on p. 140 for sprouting lentils, which can be adapted for aduki beans, alfalfa, amaranth, mung beans and quinoa.

- *Brazil nuts are a very concentrated source of selenium and eating two or three a day provides all your selenium requirements. Overdoing it isn't a good idea, so bingeing on brazil nuts isn't recommended!*

Zinc

Zinc contributes to the healthy functioning of our hormones, skin and immune systems, and our digestion. It also has anti-inflammatory properties. It is important to have small amounts each day. Plant-based sources of zinc include almonds and almond butter, asparagus, avocados, beans (especially aduki beans), bran flakes, brazil nuts, broccoli, brown rice, cacao, cashews, citrus fruits, cocoa powder/dark chocolate, dark-green leafy vegetables, garden peas, green beans, lentils, miso, mushrooms, oats, peanuts, pine nuts, pumpkin seeds, sesame seeds, sourdough, soya-based foods, spinach, sunflower seeds, tahini, tofu, wheat germ, whole grains and wholemeal bread.

Soaking nuts and seeds prior to eating them may boost the absorption of zinc, as may protein-rich and fermented foods.

Fibre

A vegan diet lends itself to obtaining adequate fibre if you are eating plenty of grains, beans and pulses, fresh fruit and root veg. If you feel you are not getting enough fibre, particularly good plant sources include: apples, black beans, broccoli, carrots, chia seeds, chickpeas, flax seeds, garden peas, lentils, oats, pearl barley, pears, quinoa, raspberries, rye flour and sweet potatoes. Of these, oats are an excellent all-round fibre-provider. Black beans, flax seeds, lentils and raspberries also help with gut health.

Drink plenty of water during the day, based on thirst, and if using chia seeds and flax seeds, allow for the fact that they absorb water when mixed with liquids.

OMEGA-6 AND OMEGA-3 ESSENTIAL FATTY ACIDS (EFAS)

The Essential Fatty Acids, Omega-6 (linolenic acid/polyunsaturated) and Omega-3 (alpha-linolenic acid/monounsaturated), are so called because they cannot be made by the body. While both fats need to be sourced from food or supplements, according to nutritionists most contemporary western diets contain an imbalance of Omega-6 and Omega-3 fats largely due to the Omega-6 fats consumed in highly processed and fried foods (from, for example, refined sunflower oil and corn oil) and may be pro-inflammatory. The ideal Omega 6:3 ratio is debated, but a ratio of around 4:1 is recommended, whereas western diets tend to have a ratio of at least 15:1 *and above*. While the EFAs are important to heart health, brain function, normal joint function and our immune systems, such distorted ratios may contribute to inflammatory diseases such as arthritis, diabetes and heart disease.

Plant-based sources of Omega-6 and Omega-3 fats in *balanced* ratios include: amaranth, avocados and avocado oil, black lentils (urad dahl), blueberries, broccoli, Brussels sprouts, butternut squash, cauliflower, chia seeds, flax seeds and flax oil, hulled hemp seeds and hemp seed oil, iceberg lettuce, kale, kidney beans, mung beans, spinach, squash, pumpkin, tropical fruit (especially papaya), walnuts and walnut oil and quinoa.

Almonds, pumpkin seeds, sesame seeds, sunflower seeds and sunflower oil are a good source of Omega-6 fats, although you don't want to eat too much of them. Organic cold-pressed sunflower oil is an alternative as it is high in monounsaturated oleic acid (Omega-9 fats, which *are* produced in the body and also found in plants such as avocados, macadamia nuts and olives). Algae and sea vegetables also provide Omega-3 fats and can be taken as a supplement.

For EFAs to be converted in the body they need to be paired with foods rich in vitamins B3, B6 and biotin (such as cabbage, cauliflower and whole grains), vitamin C and the minerals calcium, magnesium (for example, broccoli, brown rice, garden peas, leafy green vegetables and whole grains) and zinc.

SUPPLEMENTS

Although a plant-based diet is healthy and nutritious, vegans (and arguably non-vegans as well) need to take a B12 supplement. According to Jack Norris and Virginia Messina (see *Vegan for Life*, p. 89) vegans are also advised to take iodine, a lichen-based form of vitamin D3 and Omega-3 fats, either as supplements or in the form of fortified foods. The chapter 'The Vegan Food Guide' in *Vegan for Life* provides excellent guidance on vegan food groups and some nutritionally balanced sample menus.

I take Veg 1 daily, a chewable multivitamin tablet obtainable online from the Vegan Society. This contains vitamins B2, B6, B12, D3 (vegan), folic acid, selenium and iodine. I also take a vegan Omega-3 supplement twice a week and a vegan vitamin D3 tablet daily. Companies offering good vegan vitamin D3 products include Cytoplan and Viridian.

USING THIS BOOK

Prep time indicates the time it takes to bring the ingredients together, including gathering from the cupboards, washing, chopping, peeling, etc.

Cooking time indicates when heat is applied, i.e. the time it takes to cook the elements of the dish, including frying, baking, roasting, etc. Do check cooking timings and temperatures based on your knowledge of how your own oven behaves.

Where a weight is given for vegetables or fruit, this is generally the weight before trimming, peeling, coring, etc. unless otherwise stated. All fruit and vegetables should be washed before using, whether they are organic or not.

THE VEGAN STORE CUPBOARD

Listed below are the items that you may want to include in your vegan store cupboard. There is no need to buy everything at once; just pick up ingredients as you make the recipes and find your favourites. Check labels carefully as non-vegan ingredients may be used either in the foods themselves (e.g. chocolate, sauces, stock cubes) or during the production process (e.g. alcohol). Most items can be found in the supermarket or can be bought from a health-food shop.

Alcohol: I like cooking with alcohol, as it enriches and deepens the flavour of a dish (and evaporates during cooking so it is not going to make you tipsy!). I use a vegan vermouth (Sainsbury's Italian Vermouth Extra Dry) for savoury sauces and soups and would recommend having this in your cupboard, as well as a good quality whisky of course (preferably single malt) – quintessentially Scottish!

Other dishes use brandy and Muscat dessert wine, and you might want to use vegan alcohol-free white wine if you are teetotal, although you can also substitute apple juice in the same quantities.

- *Not all wine or alcohol is vegan – it depends on what is used in the fining process (often isinglass, from fish bladders, or egg whites). Vegan wines tend to use charcoal for this process. Spirits such as brandy and whisky are generally vegan unless blended with cream. To check whether or not a particular brand of alcohol is vegan, see the Barnivore website (www.barnivore.com/), which offers a guide to vegan beer, wine and liquor.*

Beans (dried or tinned): aduki beans, black beans, butter beans, chickpeas, haricot beans, red lentils, yellow split peas.

Butters: for a non-hydrogenated vegan butter alternative Vitaquell Organic Cocovit Spread is one of the few that is free from palm oil. It is made with rapeseed oil, coconut oil, shea butter, carrot juice, lemon juice, sunflower lecithin and salt. It is fine for spreading, although I find it isn't ideal for baking. Try making my home-made butter (p. 28).

With nut butters, start with your favourite, as they can be used interchangeably in most recipes. Keep nut butters in the fridge to preserve them. It is also useful to have coconut butter, which can be kept at room temperature, for solidifying some of the desserts.

Chocolate: it's useful to stock either cocoa powder or cacao powder (the former is processed, the latter raw and I tend to use the latter in desserts) and a good quality vegan dark chocolate (51% and 70% cocoa solids). Check for dairy-derived butterfat, cream and milk; 'cocoa butter' is vegan.

Cream: oat cream or soya cream are useful to keep on hand (and have a long shelf life unopened); tinned coconut milk is the basis of whipped coconut cream and an essential if you are making your own. Coconut cream and creamed coconut (refrigerate once opened) are used in some of the dessert recipes.

Dried fruit: soft or Medjool dates are an essential store cupboard item; other dried fruits used in some of the recipes are apricots (unsulphured), coconut flakes, cranberries, desiccated coconut, figs, prunes and raisins.

Dried herbs: bay leaves, oregano, rosemary, thyme.

Dried seaweed: organic arame and kombu (only if making your own stock) – obtainable from health-food shops or Asian supermarkets.

Dried spices: allspice, chilli powder, ground cardamom, ground cinnamon, ground coriander, ground cumin, ground ginger, ground mace, ground nutmeg, smoked paprika, turmeric, za'atar (a Middle Eastern herb and spice blend containing roasted sesame seeds, salt, thyme, marjoram and oregano, and sumac, a lemony spice made from ground berries).

- *Nutmeg is highly neurotoxic to dogs and should not be given to or prepared near them.*

Extracts: almond extract, vanilla extract – I use these frequently in baking and desserts.

Flours: beremeal (stoneground barley flour – can be found in health-food shops or online), chickpea (gram) flour, wholemeal plain flour, wholemeal self-raising flour, unbleached strong white (bread) flour, wholemeal spelt flour.

Grains: oats – of course! Keeping medium oatmeal and rolled oats should cover most needs; pearl barley and pudding rice are only needed if making specific recipes.

Nuts: buy as required and store in a cool, dark place. Almonds (flaked and whole), brazil nuts, cashews, hazelnuts, pecans, sweet chestnuts (dried and puréed), walnuts.

A word about . . . oil

Where possible, choose organic, cold-pressed, unrefined and non-GMO oils. Using unsaturated fats, which include monounsaturates, such as olive oil and rapeseed oil, with occasional use of polyunsaturates, such as sunflower oil, is recommended.

Cold-pressed rapeseed oil contains around half the saturated fat of olive oil, is high in mono-unsaturated fats (but not as high as olive oil), tends to have a good ratio of Omega-3 to Omega-6 acids and is a good source of vitamin E. Its beneficial antioxidants tend not to break down at high temperatures, so rapeseed oil can be used for roasting (and higher temperature cooking).

In Scotland there are now at least seven artisan brands of rapeseed oil being produced, including Ola Oils in Inverurie in Aberdeenshire and Supernature in East Lothian. My favourite is Mackintosh of Glendaveny. See www.scotrapeseedoil.co.uk for more information.

There are conflicting views about coconut oil. It is a highly saturated fat, so use sparingly – I use it in my butter recipe and occasionally for setting desserts. Use cold-pressed coconut oil and only use refined coconut oil if you need an odourless oil (i.e. in baking).

If you want to reduce the amount of oil you use altogether try roasting vegetables in water and then adding a drizzle of oil for flavour after cooking. You can also shallow fry onions and garlic, for instance, in vegan stock rather than in oil.

I usually dress a salad with a drizzle of Omega-3-rich flax seed oil, hemp seed oil or rapeseed oil and a squeeze of lemon.

Oils: my go-to all-purpose oils for low-to-mid-temperature cooking are extra virgin olive oil and cold-pressed rapeseed oil. I also keep either flax seed oil or hemp seed oil (store these in the fridge) but note that these should not be heated.

Plant milk: I keep a good stock of fortified soya milk (a good one is Milbona Unsweetened Soya Drink, with added calcium, B2, B12 and D2 from Lidl) as it contains more protein than other plant milks. My other staples are almond milk and oat milk.

Preserves: raspberry jam, stem ginger.

Raising agents: baking powder (aluminium-free), bicarbonate of soda, Easy Bake dried yeast (for baking bread).

Savoury pastes: miso paste, tomato paste.

Seasonings: the essentials are black pepper, iodised sea salt, nutritional yeast flakes (for a savoury, cheesy flavour), soy sauce/tamari (the latter is wheat-free/gluten-free), vegan bouillon powder (check there is no dairy) and yeast extract/Marmite – I am a total Marmite baby!

Nice to have and for specific recipes are: garlic granules, garlic powder, mushroom ketchup, onion powder, onion seeds, vegan worcestershire sauce (i.e. without anchovies and without soy sauce, if gluten-free; the Biona brand is both gluten-free and vegan).

Seeds: amaranth, buckwheat, chia seeds (keep in the fridge), flax seeds (keep in the fridge), hulled hemp seeds (keep in the fridge), pumpkin seeds, quinoa, sesame seeds, sunflower seeds, tahini (keep in the fridge).

Stock: Kallø organic gluten-free vegetable stock cubes; organic Swiss Vegetable (vegan) gluten-free bouillon powder.

Sweeteners: I try to use sweeteners that retain some (even if minimal) nutrients in them including:
- Barley malt extract: a natural product obtained by drying and cooking sprouted barley malt. It contains some minerals and vitamins, as well as soluble fibre. I use it when making oat milk and for baking. *Note that it is not gluten-free.*
- Blackstrap molasses: extracted as part of the process of refining sugar and retains some vital nutrients such as vitamin B6, manganese, magnesium, potassium and iron, as well as being high in calcium. I like to use it in baking.
- Coconut sugar: grown sustainably and contains vitamins B and C, iron, magnesium, potassium and zinc. I use this in baking and desserts. It doesn't taste of coconut!
- Maple syrup: retains beneficial minerals such as calcium, magnesium, manganese, potassium, riboflavin and zinc. Make sure that you buy pure Canadian maple syrup without added sweeteners.
- Muscovado sugar: unrefined cane sugar with the molasses retained. It contains some minerals such as calcium, iron and manganese.

Beetroot, carrots and sweet potatoes, and dried dates and figs can also be used as sweeteners and also contain beneficial fibre and minerals. Fruit purées are whole foods and are also a source of beneficial nutrients.

Thickening agents: agar flakes or agar powder, cornflour (ideally unbleached) (available online).

Tofu: silken tofu (a soft form of tofu/soya bean curd in a carton) (widely available).

Vinegar: apple cider vinegar, balsamic vinegar.

A word about . . . vegan honey

Vegan alternatives to honey are now becoming available commercially. I have tried an apple-based 'honee' from the US, as well as one based on rowan berries from Dalton Moor Farm in England. Grace's Pantry also makes small-batch plant-based pineapple hunnie. These can be bought online: Bee Free Honee (www.beefreehonee.com), Dalton Moor Farm Bee Free Vegan Hunny (www.alternativestores.com), Grace's Pantry (www.gracesveganpantry.com).

Another alternative to honey is Organic Coconut Blossom Nectar.

Freezer items: blackcurrants, garden peas, raspberries, vegan puff pastry.

GOING ORGANIC

While many of us try to use organic (and local, seasonal, fair trade and unpackaged) produce wherever possible, I have not specified that 'organic' fruit and vegetables should be used in the recipes given that it depends on individual preference, budget and availability in your area. If you are keen to go organic, buying seasonal fruit and veg from farmers' markets, a farm shop or a community vegetable scheme supports local producers and is likely to be less expensive, and contain less plastic packaging, than buying from a supermarket.

You may have heard about the 'Dirty Dozen' – the fruit and veg most likely to contain pesticide residues – together with the 'Clean Fifteen' – the fruit and veg most likely to contain the least pesticide residues. Each year the Environmental Working Group publishes a guide to these foods which you may want to keep in mind.

I use unwaxed lemons, limes and oranges in my recipes, given that the wax may not be vegan and may be accompanied by fungicides and pesticides. Other waxed fruit and vegetables to look out for where you would usually eat the skins include apples, aubergines, cucumbers, parsnips, peaches, peppers, sweet potatoes and turnips. Peel, wash thoroughly or scrub these in hot water before using.

Given that this is a *Scottish* cook book, I have also kept an eye on the air miles of any ingredients not grown in Scotland (e.g. bananas, cocoa, coconuts, maple syrup!). I have not excluded them; rather, I have tried to offer a balance of local and 'far (as well as fair) miles' ingredients.

BASICS

BUTTER

Makes around 250g
Prep time: 10 minutes

This buttery non-dairy butter is solid when chilled and spreadable at room temperature and can also be used for cooking and baking. I like it salted with Himalayan rose pink salt, although you can use any salt and add only half the amount if you like a less salty butter. The recipe calls for organic virgin coconut *oil* (I use Biona), which is pressed from the flesh of the coconut, and organic coconut *butter* (I use Tiana), which is pureéd coconut flesh, including the oil. The rapeseed oil provides Omega-3 fats and also gives this spread a really buttery colour.

While delicious, this non-dairy alternative to butter is high in saturated fat, so use sparingly.

INGREDIENTS

100ml unsweetened soya milk

1 teaspoon freshly squeezed lemon juice

¼ teaspoon apple cider vinegar

100g mild coconut oil, melted

50ml organic rapeseed oil

1 tablespoon organic coconut butter (at room temperature)

½–1 scant teaspoon pink Himalayan sea salt (or other salt)

2 teaspoons (non-GMO) soya lecithin granules, ground in a pestle and mortar

METHOD

In a small measuring jug, stir together the milk, lemon juice and apple cider vinegar and set aside to curdle.

To a blender jug, add the curdled milk together with the remaining ingredients and blend until the mixture has emulsified and fully combined. At this stage it will be fairly runny and golden yellow.

Pour the mixture into a bowl or into individual small square moulds (such as silicon chocolate moulds) and refrigerate for 3–4 hours before using.

This vegan butter keeps for around 2 weeks in the fridge.

CASHEW CREAM CHEESE

Prep time: 5 minutes
Cooking time:
10–15 minutes

This is a light, creamy and soft vegan cheese. It is easy to make and incredibly versatile: spread it on oatcakes or toast, use it as a sandwich filling or as a topping for a vegetable or pasta bake. See also the recipe for crowdie (p. 99) for an alternative vegan soured-cream cheese recipe.

INGREDIENTS

200g cashews

1 clove of garlic, peeled and crushed

½ teaspoon salt

1 teaspoon freshly squeezed lemon juice

½ teaspoon English mustard

Warm water, as needed

METHOD

Place the cashews in a medium pan and cover with 200ml of cold water. Bring to the boil, then reduce the heat and simmer for 10–15 minutes or until most of the water has been absorbed. Remove from the heat and cool a little.

Add the cashews and any remaining cooking liquid, garlic, salt, lemon juice and mustard to a blender and whizz until smooth and creamy. You might have to stop the blender and scrape down the sides a few times to bring everything together. Add a little more water if needed to keep the mixture moving and blend again to achieve your preferred consistency. Transfer to a bowl, cool, then cover and chill.

A word about . . . cashews

Cashews are an excellent source of protein as well as vitamins B6, E and K, and the minerals copper, iron, magnesium, phosphorus, selenium and zinc. They can be indigestible if eaten uncooked. To eliminate the enzyme inhibitors that make cashews indigestible, I simmer them until softened.

CASHEW YOGHURT

Makes around 225ml
Prep time: 10 minutes
(+ overnight chilling)
Cooking time: 10 minutes

Home-made cashew yoghurt is a lovely alternative to shop-bought vegan yoghurt, although you do need to use a little existing yoghurt for your 'starter'. I like to make quite a thick yoghurt and find this ideal for serving with fruit or fruit crumbles.

INGREDIENTS

100g cashews

150ml soya milk

1 teaspoon freshly squeezed lemon juice

1 tablespoon bioactive (i.e. containing live cultures) unsweetened, plain soya yoghurt

1½ teaspoons vanilla extract

50ml warm water

1 teaspoon maple syrup

METHOD

In a medium pan, place the cashews and cover with the milk. Bring to just below boiling, then reduce the heat and simmer for 10 minutes, stirring often.

Remove from the heat, add the lemon juice and allow the mixture to curdle and cool a little.

Place the cashew mixture, the soya yoghurt, vanilla extract, water and maple syrup in a blender jug and whizz until completely smooth, scraping down the sides as needed. Add a little more water and blend again if you prefer the consistency of your yoghurt to be thinner.

Scoop the mixture into a bowl and chill overnight. The yoghurt will keep in the fridge for 2–3 days.

A word about . . . probiotics

Yoghurt is a probiotic, a food that contains beneficial microorganisms which are good for your gut. Fermented nuts, seeds, vegetables and grains as well as soya-based foods are also helpful probiotics to add to your daily diet.

CHIA JAM

Makes approximately 100g
Prep time: 5 minutes +
setting time
Cooking time: 4–5 minutes

This quick, easy-to-make chia jam contains virtually no sugar and as such can be considered healthy compared to regular jam – and it is delicious. The beauty of the little chia seeds is that they expand when combined with liquid, including the juice from softened fruit. They add wonderful texture and also pack a big protein punch for such small things.

INGREDIENTS

100g raspberries

1 tablespoon coconut sugar

1 tablespoon cold water

¼ teaspoon vanilla extract

5–6 drops of freshly squeezed lemon juice

1 tablespoon ground chia seeds

METHOD

In a small saucepan place the raspberries, coconut sugar, water, vanilla extract and lemon juice. Cook on a low-medium heat for a few minutes, stirring with the back of a spoon to break down the raspberries into a pulp.

Take off the heat and stir in the chia seeds.

Leave to set and cool for at least 15 minutes. Keep any leftovers in the fridge and use as a topping for ice cream or on toast.

CREAM

MACADAMIA WHIPPING CREAM

Makes 200ml
Prep time: 10 minutes
(+ 3 hours' soaking time
before making and 3 hours'
chilling time)

Macadamia nuts make a perfect base for a thick, white and delectable vegan whipping cream.

INGREDIENTS

100g macadamia nuts

100ml cold water

¾ teaspoon vanilla extract

1 tablespoon coconut butter
(at room temperature)

½ tablespoon maple syrup

METHOD

In a medium bowl, place the macadamia nuts. Pour over the water and soak for up to 3 hours in the fridge.

Add the soaked nuts and the soaking water to the grinder attachment of a food processor or to a blender jug. Add the vanilla extract, coconut butter and maple syrup and pulse a few times, then process/blend until completely smooth.

Spoon the cream into a bowl and refrigerate for up to 3 hours or overnight. Remove from the fridge and before serving whip for 1–2 minutes with a hand whisk to aerate the cream. This keeps in the fridge, covered, for 2–3 days.

SOYA CREAM

Makes around 300ml
Prep time: 5 minutes
(+ chilling time)

This soya cream is like 'double' cream. It is easy to make and goes beautifully over pies, crumble and trifle.

INGREDIENTS

1 x 300g carton silken tofu, drained

2 tablespoons non-hydrogenated
vegan butter

2 tablespoons maple syrup

2 teaspoons vanilla extract

METHOD

Place all of the ingredients in a blender jug and blend until completely smooth. Scoop into a bowl and chill for several hours before using. The cream will keep in the fridge for 1–2 days.

WHIPPED COCONUT CREAM

Makes around 200ml
Prep time: 5 minutes
(+ overnight chilling
before making)

This coconut cream is thick and creamy and the ideal replacement for whipped dairy cream. Use good quality organic coconut milk if you can, as this produces a firmer whip.

INGREDIENTS

1 x 400ml tin organic coconut milk

1 teaspoon vanilla extract

2 teaspoons maple syrup or 1 teaspoon icing sugar (confectioner's sugar)

METHOD

Place the tin of coconut milk in the fridge to chill overnight or for at least 3 hours before you want to use it.

Open the tin and carefully remove only the thickened cream from the top and add it to a bowl. Set aside the remaining liquid to use in a soup or smoothie.

Add the vanilla extract and maple syrup or icing sugar and, using a balloon whisk or electric hand whisk, whip until thickened. Add a little more vanilla or sweetener, to taste. Chill until required. The cream keeps in the fridge for 2–3 days.

ICE CREAM

Makes around 500ml or
1 tub
Prep time: 5–10 minutes
(+ overnight chilling of
the coconut milk)
Churning time:
20–25 minutes

This luxurious vegan vanilla ice cream is made with oat cream, coconut cream and the seeds from a vanilla pod. The result is rich, creamy and delicious.

I've provided two options for making this – with an ice-cream maker and without!

INGREDIENTS

1 x 400ml tin coconut milk

1 x 250ml carton oat cream

1 vanilla pod, seeds scraped and pod discarded

3 tablespoons maple syrup

METHOD

Chill the coconut milk overnight and scoop just the solid cream from the top of the tin. Place this with the other ingredients in a blender and blend until completely smooth.

If using an ice-cream maker, pour the mixture into its container and churn for around 20–25 minutes until it resembles 'soft serve'. Transfer to a freezer-safe container with a lid and freeze until required. Remove from the freezer 15–20 minutes before serving to soften a little.

If you do not have an ice-cream maker, place the ice-cream mixture in a freezer-proof container with a lid, pop it in the freezer and remove and stir it thoroughly after one hour and again an hour later in order to break up the ice crystals. Freeze until required.

I like to serve this with cold Strawberry and Rhubarb Compote (p. 188), poppy seeds and coconut shavings.

KALE CRISPS AND KALE SPRINKLES

Prep time: 5 minutes
Cooking time: 6 minutes

These kale crisps are a tasty savoury snack and easy to make. You can also turn them into sprinkles and add them to soups and salads. For sprinkles, make a batch of kale crisps following the recipe below, allow them to cool and then whizz them in a blender. Store them in an air-tight jar for soup nights in winter or for salad days in summer.

INGREDIENTS

125g kale

1 tablespoon rapeseed oil

2 tablespoons sesame seeds

¼ teaspoon smoked paprika (optional)

5–6 twists of sea salt and 3–4 twists of freshly ground black pepper

METHOD

Preheat the oven to 180°C. Line a baking tray that has a rim with baking parchment.

Pull the kale from the thick stalks, tear the leaves into bite-size pieces and place them on the baking tray. Discard the stalks.

In a small bowl, mix together the other ingredients. Pour the mixture over the kale and massage it into the leaves. Ensure the leaves are coated well and spread apart for even baking.

Bake in the oven for 3 minutes, then turn with a spatula or spoon and cook for a further 3 minutes. Remove from the oven and cool before using or turning into sprinkles.

MUSHROOM GRAVY

Serves 6
Prep time: 10 minutes
Cooking time: 25 minutes

This is a thick gravy with an earthiness from the mushrooms and a hint of sweetness from the sherry. I like to serve it with a nut roast or with vegan haggis. My rich and flavoursome onion gravy (see p. 144) goes particularly well with vegan sausages or soya-based dishes.

INGREDIENTS

2 tablespoons olive oil or rapeseed oil

2 medium onions, peeled and chopped finely

2 large cloves of garlic, peeled and chopped finely

2 tablespoons vegan sherry

600g button or chestnut mushrooms, chopped finely

360ml vegan stock

1 teaspoon dried rosemary or 3 teaspoons fresh rosemary, leaves picked and chopped finely

1 teaspoon yeast extract or Marmite

150ml soya cream or oat cream

100ml hot water, if needed

METHOD

Heat the oil in a medium saucepan on a medium heat, adding the onion and sweating until softened. Add the garlic and cook for a minute, stirring. Turn up the heat and add the sherry and cook until the alcohol has evaporated (about 3 minutes).

Reduce the heat to medium, add the chopped mushrooms and cook for about 5 minutes. Next add the stock, rosemary and yeast extract or Marmite, and cook for a further 5–10 minutes.

Remove from the heat and blend the gravy in the pan with a hand-held blender until smooth, before stirring in the cream. Keep on a low heat until required (do not allow the sauce to boil once the soya cream has been added).

To serve, add hot water, if needed, to thin the sauce to your preferred pouring consistency and bring gently to serving temperature. If you have any left over, allow it to cool completely and refrigerate it. It will keep for a couple of days and can be reheated in a pan on a low-to-medium heat with a little water or soya milk.

OAT MILK

Makes around 600ml
Prep time: 10 minutes (+ 30 minutes soaking time)

While you can buy ready-prepared cartons of oat milk, it is easy (if a bit messy) to make your own. Use in porridge, on breakfast cereals, in smoothies and in recipes which call for oat milk!

You can use rolled oats or certified gluten-free oats in the same proportions (oats may be cross-contaminated with gluten in the manufacturing process and some people are also allergic to avenin, the glutinous protein found in oats).

You will need either a nut-milk bag or piece of fine-meshed muslin for straining the mixture.

INGREDIENTS

100g rolled oats + soaking water

500ml cold water

A pinch of salt

METHOD

Place the oats in a medium bowl, cover with cold water to about 3cm above and chill in the fridge.

After 30 minutes, drain off any soaking water (set aside the bowl), rinse the oats in cold water, then place them in a blender jug. Add the 500ml of cold water and blend on high speed until thoroughly combined.

Next, pass the oat mixture through a nut-milk bag or a piece of muslin into the bowl in which you soaked the oats, squeezing to extract all of the creamy milk (discard the oat pulp). Stir in the salt, transfer to a jug and refrigerate until needed.

This keeps for around 5 days in the fridge. You will need to stir the milk to recombine it each time you use it. If you prefer a thicker milk, use less water at the blending stage.

A word about . . . oats

Oats and oatmeal are at the heart of Scottish cookery and play a starring role in this book. Not only are oats and oatmeal versatile – they are used to make milk, cream, porridge, bread, burgers and crumble – they also have numerous nutritional benefits. They are a source of carbohydrates and protein, they are packed with soluble fibre, they are rich in vitamins B1 and B6 and in the minerals calcium, iron, magnesium, potassium and zinc, as well as folic acid, and they can help reduce cholesterol and lower the risk of heart disease. They are also a good source of tryptophan (see p. 13).

SAVOURY SHORTCRUST PASTRY

Makes 300g (enough for
1 tart base)
Prep time: 15 minutes
Cooking time: 10 minutes
or 20–25 minutes

It is satisfying to make your own shortcrust pastry every so often, so here is a really straightforward recipe if you don't already have a tried-and-tested one to hand. The key to success is to have cold hands and not to overwork the pastry! This recipe is inspired by the Cranks recipe for wholemeal shortcrust pastry, which uses nut butter.

INGREDIENTS

150g organic plain wholemeal flour

A pinch of salt

2 tablespoons almond butter
(fridge-cold)

2 tablespoons olive oil

Fridge-cold water to bind

METHOD

Preheat the oven to 180°C.

In a medium mixing bowl sieve together the flour and the salt. Add the almond butter and olive oil, and rub it into the flour mixture with the tips of your fingers until it resembles fine breadcrumbs.

Adding a tablespoon of cold water at a time, bring the pastry together into a firm ball with your hands. Wrap in baking parchment and refrigerate for at least 30 minutes.

Remove the pastry from the fridge, place it on a floured board or cold surface and roll it with a rolling pin dusted with flour to a size slightly larger than your pie dish.

Drape the pastry over a floured rolling pin and slide in onto the pie dish from the centre, pressing it gently into the dish and easing it up the sides. Cut away any overhanging pastry by running a sharp knife held at a diagonal angle around the top edge of the dish. Prick the base with a fork.

If adding a filling which needs to be cooked or heated, bake the base in the preheated oven for 10 mins, remove and add the filling, and proceed to finish cooking as required.

If adding a cold filling, bake the base in the preheated oven for 20–25 minutes until it is golden and cool completely before adding the filling.

TOMATO KETCHUP

Makes around 600ml
Prep time: 10 minutes
Cooking time: 35–40
minutes (mostly unattended)

It is easy to reach for the brand-name, shop-bought ketchup or an organic alternative, and I often do, but once in a while it is fun to make a home-made version. This flavoursome ketchup does have a daunting list of ingredients, although they are mostly dried spices. Just line them up on your work surface before you start and measure carefully!

INGREDIENTS

1 tablespoon olive oil or rapeseed oil

2 shallots or small onions, peeled and chopped finely

1 celery stick, trimmed and sliced finely

1 clove of garlic, peeled and crushed

1 x 400g tin chopped tomatoes

1 heaped tablespoon tomato purée mixed with 3 tablespoons hot water

300ml cold water

½ tablespoon apple cider vinegar

½ teaspoon dried mixed herbs

½ teaspoon ground coriander

½ teaspoon ground cumin

½ teaspoon ground ginger

¼ teaspoon ground allspice

¼ teaspoon ground nutmeg

¼ teaspoon celery salt

4 cloves

Freshly ground black pepper

2 pitted Medjool dates, chopped finely

1 tablespoon dark muscovado sugar

Salt

METHOD

In a medium saucepan with a lid, heat the oil gently, add the onion and celery and sweat until softened. Then add the garlic and cook for a minute, stirring.

Next, stir in the tinned tomatoes, tomato purée mixture, water and apple cider vinegar and bring to the boil.

Reduce the heat, add the mixed herbs, coriander, cumin, ginger, allspice, nutmeg, celery salt, cloves, 3–4 twists of pepper, the dates and the muscovado sugar and give it all a good stir. Simmer, partially covered, for 30 minutes, stirring occasionally. Taste and season further, if liked, with salt and black pepper. Remove from the heat and cool.

Remove the cloves with a spoon, add the sauce to a blender jug or use a hand-held blender and whizz until smooth. If the sauce is a little too thick, add a little water and blend again. Pour into an air-tight jar and chill. The sauce will keep in the fridge for up to 2 weeks.

VANILLA CUSTARD

Makes 500ml
Prep time: 5 minutes
Cooking time: 6–8 minutes

It's handy to have a vegan vanilla custard recipe for smothering over any kind of steamed pudding, crumble or fruit pie. Soya milk definitely makes the best custard, as it thickens better than other plant milks.

INGREDIENTS

4 tablespoons cornflour

500ml unsweetened soya milk

2 teaspoons vanilla extract

1½ tablespoons maple syrup
(and extra, if needed)

METHOD

In a small bowl, mix the cornflour together with 8 tablespoons of soya milk. Set aside.

In a medium saucepan, combine the remaining soya milk, vanilla extract and maple syrup. Bring to a medium-high heat, stirring regularly to ensure the milk does not boil or catch on the bottom of the pan.

When almost at boiling point, turn down the heat to low, pour some of the milk into the bowl containing the cornflour mixture and stir quickly, then add the cornflour mixture back into the milk in the pan. Stir continuously until the custard thickens, adding a little more maple syrup if needed to suit your taste.

VEGAN STOCK

Makes 1 litre
Prep time: 20 minutes
Cooking time:
45–50 minutes

Although there are some great low-salt, vegan (and gluten-free) stock cubes, stock powders and ready-made vegetable bouillons available, nothing beats a freshly made vegetable stock on occasions to give wonderful flavour to a soup or stew.

INGREDIENTS

2 medium onions, peeled and chopped roughly

2 medium leeks, trimmed and chopped roughly (about 250g prepped)

2 celery sticks, trimmed and chopped roughly

2 large carrots, scrubbed or peeled, trimmed and chopped roughly

1½ litres of cold water

2 bay leaves

6 peppercorns

¼ teaspoon dried thyme or ¾ teaspoon fresh thyme, leaves picked and chopped finely

METHOD

In a medium saucepan place all of the vegetables, cover with the water, add the bay leaves, peppercorns and thyme and bring to the boil.

Then turn down the heat and simmer, uncovered, until the vegetables are all cooked (about 45 minutes). Drain the liquid through a sieve or colander into a heat-proof bowl and discard the vegetables as they have served their purpose.

Use as per your recipe or allow to cool and then refrigerate and use within 2–3 days. You can also freeze the stock once cooled in ½-litre freezer-proof containers and defrost and use when needed. This keeps for a good few months.

BREAKFAST & BRUNCH

BAKED GRAPEFRUIT, ORANGE AND RASPBERRY BOWL

Serves 2
Prep time: 5 minutes
Cooking time: 20 minutes

This quick and easy recipe is slightly retro! It reminds me of fruit cocktail, although it is served warm for a delectable breakfast or brunch. It is equally good served cold. If you are not a fan of grapefruit, you might be converted by this recipe!

INGREDIENTS

1 large pink grapefruit, peeled, pith and pips removed and cut into segments

1 large orange, peeled, pith and pips removed and cut into segments

100g raspberries

2 star anise

1 tablespoon maple syrup

1 teaspoon vanilla extract

TO SERVE

Hulled hemp seeds

METHOD

Preheat the oven to 180°C.

In a medium-size ovenproof dish, place the grapefruit and orange segments, the raspberries and the star anise.

In a small bowl, mix together the maple syrup and vanilla extract. Spoon this over the fruit and combine carefully.

Bake in the oven for 10 minutes, then stir gently and place back in the oven to cook for a further 10 minutes. Remove from the oven and cool a little. To serve, arrange in fruit cocktail glasses or bowls, sprinkle with hemp seeds and add a dollop of vegan yoghurt.

A word about . . . grapefruit

Grapefruit is amazing! Not only is it a source of vitamin C, it also contains lycopene, a powerful antioxidant which helps maintain the health of our cell membranes. Other sources of lycopene include papaya, tomatoes and watermelon. *A word of warning, however.* Grapefruit is contra-indicated with many medications, as it affects liver enzyme function quite dramatically. This is usually mentioned in the information sheets that come with the drugs, so do check if you are on medication.

A word about . . . hemp seeds

Hulled hemp seeds provide Omega-3 and Omega-6 fats in a balanced ratio, as well as protein, vitamin E, magnesium, manganese, copper, iron and zinc. Although they are an expensive item they are a nutritional powerhouse. They keep well in the fridge for weeks. Hemp seeds, by the way, contain no psycho-active ingredients.

BLACK BEAN AND MUSHROOM 'BLACK PUDDING'

Makes 8 puddings
Prep time: 15 minutes
Cooking time: 45 minutes

This is a delicious and healthier vegan version of a cherished Scottish savoury breakfast item! The black beans provide excellent protein, yeast extract/Marmite is usually fortified with vitamin B12, and the mushrooms are rich in vitamin D and also contain protein. The black puddings can be prepared the night before, if you prefer, refrigerated once cooled and cooked the next day once brought to room temperature.

INGREDIENTS

2 tablespoons olive oil or rapeseed oil

1 medium onion, peeled and chopped finely

3 cloves of garlic, peeled and crushed

150g chestnut mushrooms or button mushrooms, chopped finely

1 x 400g tin black beans, drained (net weight 240g), rinsed and mashed

1 teaspoon yeast extract or Marmite mixed with 100ml hot water

1 teaspoon dried thyme or 3 teaspoons fresh thyme, leaves picked and chopped finely

1 teaspoon dried oregano or 3 teaspoons fresh oregano, chopped finely

¼ teaspoon ground mace

1 tablespoon vegan medium dry sherry

A squeeze of fresh lemon

A small bunch of parsley, chopped finely to make 2 heaped tablespoons

Salt and freshly ground black pepper

55g rolled oats

Olive oil or rapeseed oil for cooking

METHOD

Preheat the oven to 180°C. Line a baking tray with baking parchment.

In a medium, heavy-based frying pan, heat the oil on medium heat, add the onion and sweat until softened. Add the garlic and cook for a minute, stirring. Then add the mushrooms and cook for 3–4 minutes.

Next, stir in the mashed beans, yeast extract/Marmite mixture, the thyme, oregano, mace, sherry and lemon juice, and cook for a further 6–8 minutes or until the liquid has evaporated (you want the mixture to be sticky and firm rather than wet). Stir in the parsley and season to taste with salt and black pepper.

Remove the pan from the heat, stir in the oats and mix until thoroughly combined. Taste again and season further, if necessary. Allow the mixture to cool slightly before shaping into puddings; if it is a little wet, add a few more oats.

Take a handful of the mixture and mould it with your hands into a round, flat pudding about 2½cm thick. Repeat with the rest of the mixture. If you are making the puddings in advance, stop here, place on a plate, cover and put in the fridge until needed.

If eating immediately, in a large frying pan, heat a little oil on a medium heat. Add as many puddings as will fit, while leaving a little space between them, and cook on each side for around 3–4 minutes. As you fry them, place the puddings on the prepared baking tray and once you have fried them all, bake them in the preheated oven for about 8 minutes, turn them, and cook for a further 7 minutes.

Serve with 'Tattie' Scones (p. 68) and Tomato Ketchup (p. 41) or with 'Stovies' (p. 155). For a lighter meal, serve with a tomato salad made from two large tomatoes, chopped and mixed with a tablespoon of hulled hemp seeds, finely chopped oregano, mint and parsley, a little hemp oil, a squeeze of fresh lemon, and salt and black pepper to taste.

BLUEBERRY AND OAT MILK SMOOTHIE

Serves 2
Prep time: 5 minutes

This creamy smoothie provides a nourishing start to the day. It's also a great after-exercise recovery drink. Use your home-made oat milk – see the recipe (p. 39), which includes a gluten-free option – or a shop-bought version such as Rude Health, which is gluten-free, or Alpro, which is fortified with vitamin B12, D and calcium.

INGREDIENTS

300ml cold oat milk

100g blueberries

½ banana, peeled and sliced

3 tablespoons chilled soya yoghurt

½ teaspoon vanilla extract

1 soft, pitted date, chopped finely (optional)

TO SERVE

Freshly grated or ground nutmeg

METHOD

Place all of the ingredients into a blender and blend until thick and smooth. Pour into tall glasses, sprinkle with a little nutmeg and drink straightaway.

DATE, ALMOND MILK AND PEANUT BUTTER BLISS SHAKE

Serves 2
Prep time: 5 minutes

Just three ingredients go into this heavenly shake.

INGREDIENTS

3 pitted Medjool dates, chopped finely

300ml cold, unsweetened almond milk

2 tablespoons smooth, unsweetened peanut butter

METHOD

Place all of the ingredients in a blender jug and whizz until smooth and the dates have all been incorporated. Pour into two glasses and drink straightaway.

CARROT 'CAKE' BREAKFAST BOWL

Serves 2–4
Prep time: 10 minutes
(+ overnight soaking)

This is one of my favourite Scottish oat-based breakfasts and always feels decadent. It's like eating carrot cake first thing in the morning! Prepare the night before for a ready-made bowl of healthy scrumptiousness.

INGREDIENTS

50g rolled oats

1 medium carrot, scrubbed or peeled and grated

Zest and juice of half a medium orange (set aside a little zest for decorating)

2 dried figs, chopped

200ml oat milk or other plant milk

3 walnuts, chopped roughly

¼ teaspoon ground cinnamon

¼ teaspoon ground mixed spice

A pinch of salt

1 teaspoon maple syrup or blackstrap molasses

TO SERVE

1 teaspoon hulled hemp seeds

1 tablespoon unsweetened coconut flakes

orange zest

METHOD

Place all of the ingredients (except the hemp seeds, coconut flakes and reserved orange zest) in a medium bowl in the order given and mix together thoroughly. Chill in the fridge overnight.

To serve, spoon into breakfast bowls, sprinkle over the hemp seeds, coconut flakes and orange zest, and enjoy!

CRUNCHY OATS

Makes 275g
Prep time: 10 minutes
Cooking time: 8–10 minutes

By baking your own oats with nuts and seeds you can easily create a wonderful crunchy cereal full of heart healthiness, as well as control how sweet you would like it.

INGREDIENTS

150g rolled oats

25g hazelnuts, chopped roughly

25g almonds, chopped roughly

25g dried apricots, chopped roughly

40g pitted Medjool dates, chopped roughly

20g coconut flakes or coconut chips, chopped roughly

1 piece of stem ginger, chopped finely

½ teaspoon ground cinnamon

A pinch of salt

1–2 tablespoons maple syrup or vegan honey

2 tablespoons coconut oil (melted) or olive oil

METHOD

Preheat the oven to 180°C.

Line a baking tray with baking parchment. Spread the oats on the tray, then scatter the hazelnuts, almonds, apricot and date pieces, the coconut and the stem ginger over the oats. Sprinkle over the cinnamon and salt and drizzle over the sweetener and oil. Mix everything together thoroughly with a spoon.

Place in the preheated oven for 4–5 minutes. Then stir and cook for a further 4–5 minutes or until golden brown. Remove from the oven, cool completely and store in an airtight container.

Serve with cashew yoghurt (p. 30) or with your favourite vegan yoghurt, fresh blueberries and slices of banana.

EASY KALE, TOMATO AND CASHEW NUT STIR-UP

Serves 2
Prep time: 5 minutes
Cooking time:
10–12 minutes

This dish is so quick and easy to prepare. It is also highly nourishing: the cooked tomatoes provide vitamin C and lycopene and the cashews are a good source of protein, magnesium, iron and vitamin B6.

INGREDIENTS

2 tablespoons rapeseed oil or avocado oil

2 large garlic cloves, peeled and crushed

200g cherry tomatoes, halved

80g cashews

200g kale, thick stalks removed and chopped finely

2 tablespoons tomato purée mixed with 5 tablespoons hot water

Salt and freshly ground black pepper

1 teaspoon ground nutmeg

METHOD

In a heavy-based pan heat the oil on medium-high heat. Add the garlic and fry for a minute, stirring. Then add the cherry tomatoes and cashews and cook them for 3–4 minutes, stirring often. Next, add the kale and the tomato purée mixture, salt, pepper and nutmeg and cook for 6–7 minutes or until the kale has wilted and is tender. Serve on wholemeal, rye or sourdough toast.

A word about . . . kale

Kale has long been a part of the Scottish diet, especially in the past among people who worked the land. It has risen to fame in recent years as a super food and for good reason: kale contains a range of vitamins and minerals including calcium, copper, folate, iron, magnesium, manganese, phosphorus, potassium, riboflavin, thiamin, vitamin A, vitamin B6, vitamin C and vitamin K!

Kale is an excellent calcium booster: one cup of raw kale contains around 137mg of calcium and a little over 90mg when cooked.

LORNE 'SAUSAGE'

Serves 4–6
Prep time: 20 minutes
(+ 1–2 hours chilling time)
Cooking time: 6–8 minutes,
or 20–25 minutes, if baking
in the oven

A traditional Scottish square breakfast sausage, it is usually made from crushed meat and rusk, shaped in a tin and then sliced. It is said to be named after the ancient district of Lorne in Argyll in the west of Scotland. My husband, Sandy, says Lorne sausage was a big favourite in his home town of Mauchline (famed for small wooden boxes known as 'Mauchline ware', clock-making, the only curling stone factory in the world, and an association with the Scottish poet Robert Burns) and was bought from the 'chippy'.

My vegan version uses black-eyed beans and kidney beans, wholemeal breadcrumbs and traditional seasoning – and apparently it comes close to the original! Prepare ahead, as the mixture needs to be chilled in order to hold its shape.

INGREDIENTS

1 x 400g tin black-eyed beans, drained (240g net weight), rinsed in cold water

1 x 400g tin kidney beans, drained (240g net weight), rinsed in cold water

1 teaspoon olive oil or rapeseed oil

2 shallots, peeled and chopped finely

1 teaspoon ground nutmeg

¼ teaspoon ground mace

1 teaspoon ground coriander

2 teaspoons vegan stock powder

Salt and freshly ground black pepper

125g wholemeal vegan breadcrumbs, toasted

1 flax seed egg (1 tablespoon ground flax seeds mixed with 3 tablespoons cold water and set aside for a few minutes to thicken)

Olive oil or rapeseed oil for cooking

METHOD

Line an 18cm x 26cm shallow tin with biodegradable cling film so that it comes over all of the sides. Set aside.

In a medium bowl, mash the black-eyed beans and kidney beans with the oil.

Stir in the chopped shallots, nutmeg, mace, coriander and stock powder and season with salt and black pepper to taste.

Add the breadcrumbs and flax seed egg and mix together thoroughly with your hands, squeezing the mixture together to make it as compact as possible.

Scoop the mixture into the tin. With the back of a spoon press it down evenly and firmly into the sides and edges and then cover with the overhanging cling film. Place in the fridge for 1–2 hours.

Remove the mixture from the fridge, turn it out of the tin and cut into large square slices, having removed and recycled the cling film.

In a large frying pan, heat a little oil on medium heat and shallow fry the sausage slices for 5–6 minutes on each side or until golden brown and cooked through. Alternatively, bake in a preheated oven at 180°C for 20–25 minutes, turning once halfway through, until browned and crisp on the outsides.

Serve in a Morning Roll (p. 117) with Tomato Ketchup (p. 41) or with a leafy green side salad.

OATMEAL AND TOASTED SEEDS

Serves 2
Prep time: 10 minutes
(+ overnight soaking)
Cooking time:
10–15 minutes

Although traditionally made in Scotland with water and salt, I prefer to use soya milk fortified with calcium in oatmeal for an extra health boost. Use finely ground oatmeal for a lovely bowl of creamy richness.

INGREDIENTS

75g fine oatmeal

500ml soya milk

A pinch of salt

20g pumpkin seeds

20g sesame seeds

1 medium banana, peeled and sliced

2 teaspoons blackstrap molasses

METHOD

In a medium bowl, place the oatmeal and pour over 250ml of the soya milk. Stir well, cover, and chill overnight.

In the morning add the oatmeal mixture to a medium saucepan. Pour over the remaining 250ml of soya milk and add the salt, bring to medium heat and cook until creamy (about 10 minutes), stirring most of the time to avoid the oatmeal sticking to the bottom of the pan.

In a small frying pan dry-fry the pumpkin and sesame seeds until the pumpkin seeds pop.

When the porridge is ready, ladle into warm bowls, add the banana slices, drizzle over the blackstrap molasses and top with the toasted seeds.

PORRIDGE WITH BLUEBERRIES, HAZELNUTS AND WHEAT GERM

Serves 2
Prep time: 5 minutes
Cooking time: 8–10 minutes

The addition of wheat germ to heart-healthy porridge oats provides a lovely nuttiness as well as extra nutrition, so if you are not yet into wheat germ, it's worth giving it a go! Traditionally, Scottish porridge (as well as broth, soups and stews) is stirred with an implement known as a 'spurtle' – a stick of wood shaped like a rod – but a wooden spoon will do! This thick, creamy porridge will set you up for the day.

INGREDIENTS

60g rolled oats

30g wheat germ

30g hazelnuts, whole

100g blueberries

A pinch of salt

230ml unsweetened soya milk or other plant milk

TO SERVE

1 pear or apple, unpeeled, cored and sliced

2 tablespoons hulled hemp seeds

Maple syrup, to serve

METHOD

In a small saucepan place all of the ingredients and mix together. Cook on low-medium heat (do not allow to boil), stirring continuously until the blueberries have turned the porridge a lovely purple colour and the oats are creamy – about 8–10 minutes. Add a little more milk at this point, if liked, and bring to serving temperature.

Remove from the heat, divide between two bowls and serve with slices of pear or apple, a sprinkle of hulled hemp seeds and a drizzle of maple syrup.

A word about . . . wheat germ

Wheat germ forms a tiny part of a whole grain of wheat. Although small, it is full of goodness, including the B vitamins thiamin, riboflavin, niacin, vitamin B6, folate and pantothenic acid, vitamin E, the minerals calcium, iron, magnesium, phosphorous, potassium, sodium and zinc, and the trace minerals copper, manganese and selenium, as well as Omega-3 and Omega-6 fats. The omegas are in a ratio of about 1:8, so include a source of Omega-3 (such as hulled hemp seeds) alongside wheat germ. Wheat germ is available from health-food shops (e.g. Holland and Barrett) and online. Add wheat germ to porridge, oatmeal and overnight oats, sprinkle over breakfast cereals or stir into smoothies for nutty-flavoured extra nutrition.

QUINOA, FRUIT AND NUT NUTRIENT BOWL

Serves 2
Prep time: 10 minutes +
overnight chilling

This scrumptious brunch bowl contains an abundance of nutrients. It is quick to prepare the night before, then just add your preferred toppings in the morning. If you can, use soya milk fortified with B12.

INGREDIENTS

2 tablespoons ground chia seeds

2 tablespoons quinoa flakes

4 brazil nuts, grated

2 dried figs, chopped

1 tablespoon almond butter

1 tablespoon cacao powder (or cocoa powder) (optional)

¼ teaspoon ground cinnamon

A pinch of salt

1 teaspoon blackstrap molasses

250ml unsweetened soya milk

1 teaspoon vanilla extract

METHOD

In a medium bowl place all the ingredients and mix them together thoroughly. Chill in the fridge overnight. The following morning, spoon into bowls and I like to scatter blueberries, strawberries and hulled hemp seeds on top.

SCOTCH PANCAKES WITH RHUBARB AND APPLE COMPOTE

Makes around 16 pancakes
Prep time: 10 minutes
Cooking time:
5 minutes per batch

Scotch pancakes are small and thick rather than large and thin like a French crêpe or an English pancake. They are more often eaten at teatime, although they make a great brunch option too. I have suggested serving them here with Rhubarb and Apple Compote, but they go just as well with savoury toppings.

INGREDIENTS FOR THE PANCAKES

150ml soya milk or other plant milk

1 teaspoon apple cider vinegar

1 teaspoon vanilla extract

1 teaspoon maple syrup or vegan honey

1 teaspoon olive oil or rapeseed oil

100g organic wholemeal plain flour

1½ teaspoons baking powder

A pinch of salt

50ml cold sparkling water

Rapeseed oil or avocado oil to cook the pancakes

METHOD

In a jug, stir together the soya milk, apple cider vinegar, vanilla extract, maple syrup or vegan honey and the oil. Set aside to curdle.

In a medium-size mixing bowl, bring together the flour, baking powder and salt.

Next, add the soya milk mixture to the flour mixture and stir until well combined. Then stir in the sparkling water. For Scotch pancakes, the batter should be quite thick.

In a large, non-stick frying pan heat a little oil to a high heat (swirl the oil around to thinly coat the whole pan). Ladle a tablespoon of batter per pancake into the pan, fitting 4–6 pancakes in at the same time (depending on the size of your frying pan).

Cook each pancake on one side until bubbles start to appear on the surface (around 2½ minutes), then flip with a spatula and cook for a further 2½ minutes on the other side, or until golden brown and cooked through. Either serve the pancakes as you make them or keep them warm while you prepare the next batch. Add a very little oil to the pan each time.

RHUBARB AND APPLE COMPOTE

Prep time: 5 minutes
Cooking time: 15 minutes

If you want to get ahead, you can make the compote the day before, cool and chill it and either re-warm it in a saucepan the next day or serve it cold. It will keep for 2–3 days in the fridge and any leftovers make a lovely topping for porridge.

INGREDIENTS

5–6 pitted soft dates, chopped finely

300g rhubarb, trimmed and chopped roughly

1 cooking apple, such as Bramley, peeled, cored and chopped roughly

1 star anise

½ teaspoon ground cinnamon

METHOD

Place the dates in a medium saucepan and cover them with cold water. Bring to a boil, then reduce the heat and simmer for 5 minutes, stirring. Add the remaining ingredients to the pan and continue to simmer, stirring now and again, until the fruit has turned to a pulp – about another 10 minutes.

Remove from the heat and take out the star anise with a spoon. Pass the mixture through a sieve and discard any remaining pulp.

SCRAMBLED TOFU

Serves 2–4
Prep time: 20 minutes
Cooking time: 10 minutes

Scrambled tofu is a super-healthy, protein-packed, calcium-rich, yummy vegan brunch dish! This recipe brings out the best in tofu, with the cashews adding both protein and texture. This is a tasty way to test out tofu if you or your fellow diners are new to it. It also packs in a few colourful veggies for goodness.

INGREDIENTS

2 tablespoons olive oil or rapeseed oil

1 onion, peeled and sliced finely

1 medium carrot, scrubbed or peeled, and grated

1 celery stick, trimmed and chopped finely

8–10 cherry tomatoes, halved, or 3–4 medium tomatoes, quartered

1 clove of garlic, peeled and sliced finely

200g organic firm tofu, gently pressed in a sieve to remove any excess water

½ teaspoon ground turmeric

¼ teaspoon celery seed

2 teaspoons tomato purée dissolved in 2 tablespoons hot water

¼ teaspoon dark muscovado sugar (optional)

40g cashews

70g spinach leaves or kale (thick stems removed)

A small bunch of fresh chives, chopped finely

Salt and freshly ground black pepper

½ tablespoon sesame seeds

METHOD

In a medium frying pan or saucepan, heat the oil on medium heat and sweat the onion, carrot and celery until softened. Add the tomatoes and garlic and cook for a minute, stirring.

Crumble in the tofu and combine it thoroughly with the vegetables.

Add the turmeric, celery seed, tomato purée, the sugar if using (it takes away any tartness from the cooked tomatoes), the cashews and the spinach and cook on medium heat for around 5 minutes, stirring occasionally and adding a little water if necessary to keep the mixture moving.

Stir in the chives, keeping some back to sprinkle on top, and then season to taste with salt and black pepper.

Serve straightaway on sourdough toast and sprinkle with sesame seeds and extra chopped chives.

SUPER BREKKIE JUICES

SUPER GREEN JUICE

Serves 1–2
Prep time: 5 minutes

This juice really is super: the spinach and watercress provide iron, as well as vitamins A, C and K and the minerals calcium, magnesium and manganese. The peas are a source of protein and the ginger adds some vitamin C, copper and potassium to this vibrant green concoction.

INGREDIENTS

A large handful of fresh or frozen spinach

A small handful of watercress

7cm piece of cucumber, peeled and chopped roughly

50g frozen garden peas

1 celery stick, trimmed and grated

2cm piece of root ginger, peeled and grated finely

A few stalks of parsley

Some mint leaves

3 tablespoons elderflower cordial

250ml cold water

Hulled hemp seeds

METHOD

Place all of the ingredients except the hemp seeds in a blender jug and whizz until thoroughly combined and ultra-smooth. To serve, pour into a tall glass or share between two small glasses, sprinkle some hemp seeds over the top and drink straightaway.

CARROT JUICE SMOOTHIE

Serves 1–2
Prep time: 5 minutes

This drink is like a meal in a glass. With just five plant ingredients, it is quick to prepare and also pretty good for you!

INGREDIENTS

150ml carrot juice

50ml oat milk or other plant milk

1 medium ripe banana, peeled and sliced

5cm piece of root ginger, peeled, grated

1 tablespoon unsweetened soya yoghurt or other vegan yoghurt

TO SERVE

A handful of sesame seeds or pumpkin seeds

METHOD

First squeeze the grated ginger in your hands to make 15 drops of ginger juice (discard the remaining ginger pulp).

Place all of the ingredients in a blender jug and blend until smooth. Pour into one tall glass, or two small glasses, sprinkle with the seeds, and drink straightaway.

'TATTIE' SCONES

Makes 8 scones
Prep time: 25 minutes
Cooking time: 8–12 minutes

'Tattie' scones are a classic round, flat savoury pancake made with mashed potato and are nothing like the kind of baked sweet scones traditionally eaten with cream and jam! They are a staple of the 'full Scottish' or cooked breakfast, although they pair well with Scrambled Tofu (p. 64) and even with marmalade!

INGREDIENTS

285g floury potatoes (such as King Edward or Maris Piper)

1 teaspoon olive oil or rapeseed oil

2 tablespoons unsweetened soya milk or other plant milk

¼ teaspoon salt

Freshly ground black pepper

50g organic unbleached plain flour or quinoa flour + extra for dusting and rolling

¼ teaspoon baking powder

Olive oil or rapeseed oil to cook

METHOD

Peel the potatoes and cut them into quarters. In a medium saucepan, boil the potatoes until softened but not disintegrating (about 8–10 minutes), then drain away the water. Mash the potato with the oil, soya milk, salt and a couple of twists of black pepper.

Add the flour and baking powder to the mash and combine thoroughly.

Divide the mixture in two. Turn one half of the mixture out onto a floured board or surface and sprinkle the top with flour. With a floured rolling pin, roll out to form a circle around 5mm thickness and cut into quarters. Set aside. Repeat with the second half of the mixture.

In a medium non-stick frying pan, heat a very little oil on medium-high heat. Add the potato scones in two separate batches and cook them for 2–3 minutes on each side or until golden brown. Keep the first batch warm while making the second.

These are best eaten the same day or can be eaten cold.

TEMPEH BUTTY

Serves 2
Prep time: 15 minutes
(+ 30 minutes' marinating time)
Cooking time: 35 minutes

This is my vegan take on the bacon roll or bacon butty. It uses marinated tempeh and lots of onions and is seriously mouth-watering, as well as full of healthy ingredients, from the protein in the mushrooms to the calcium-rich tahini and the vitamins (B, E and K) and folic acid in the miso!

INGREDIENTS

3 tablespoons tahini

2 tablespoons cold water

1 tablespoon miso

1 teaspoon freshly squeezed lemon juice

1 tablespoon tamari

1 tablespoon maple syrup

2–3 twists of black pepper

200g of fresh tempeh (keep in the fridge until ready to use), sliced into thick strips

2 tablespoons olive oil or rapeseed oil, divided

3 onions, peeled and sliced into rings

8 mushrooms, sliced finely

2 cloves of garlic, peeled and crushed

METHOD

In a medium bowl, mix together the tahini, water, miso, lemon juice, tamari, maple syrup and pepper. Add the strips of tempeh and marinate for 25–30 minutes.

Meanwhile, to a medium saucepan or frying pan on medium heat add 1 tablespoon of the oil and the onions. Sweat for about 20–25 minutes until they have caramelised. Keep on a low heat until ready to serve.

Once the tempeh strips have finished marinating, in a separate frying pan gently heat the remaining tablespoonful of oil. Stir in the sliced mushrooms and cook for 5–6 minutes. Add the garlic and cook for a minute or so, stirring.

Add the marinated tempeh strips and fry for 3–4 minutes on each side.

Serve the tempeh 'bacon' and mushrooms in a roll with a generous portion of the fried onions and a dollop of Tomato Ketchup (p. 41) or shop-bought sauce.

For a more substantial meal, serve with cooked amaranth or quinoa, steamed broccoli and garden peas.

A word about . . . tempeh

Tempeh is made from fermented whole soya beans. It is stronger in flavour, firmer and chewier than tofu, even a bit yeasty, and is an excellent source of protein and fibre, as well as B vitamins, calcium, iron, magnesium and zinc.

Tempeh contains an edible white mould called mycelia as a result of the culturing process. You can buy tempeh fresh or frozen from health-food shops. Always refrigerate fresh tempeh and use it within a week.

VANILLA POTS WITH WARM BLACKBERRY SAUCE

Serves 2
Prep time: 10 minutes (+ overnight soaking)
Cooking time: 5 minutes (7–8, if cooking from frozen)

These little pots contain just a handful of ingredients yet pack a great protein punch from the chia seeds and soya milk. The blackberry sauce adds a gorgeous flavour, as well as vitamin C. You can also use blueberries or raspberries for the sauce, if blackberries are hard to come by.

INGREDIENTS FOR THE VANILLA POTS

2 tablespoons ground chia seeds

150ml unsweetened soya milk

1 teaspoon vanilla extract

INGREDIENTS FOR THE WARM BLACKBERRY SAUCE

80g fresh or frozen blackberries

3 tablespoons water (2 tablespoons, if cooking from frozen)

1 teaspoon vanilla extract

1 tablespoon maple syrup

TO SERVE

1 tablespoon plain or vanilla vegan yoghurt

Pumpkin seeds

METHOD

Start the vanilla pots by placing the chia seeds in a medium bowl, adding the milk and the vanilla extract, and stirring until the chia seeds begin to thicken. Divide the chia mixture between two small pots or bowls and chill overnight.

In the morning, prepare the blackberry sauce. In a small saucepan, place all of the ingredients and bring to a slow simmer on a medium heat. Stir often, pressing the blackberries with the back of a spoon to ensure they break up. When the liquid has been reduced and the blackberries are beginning to turn 'jammy', remove from the heat and pass the blackberries through a sieve into a bowl, leaving the pips behind, which can be discarded.

Spoon the sauce generously over the vanilla mixture. Finish with a swirl of yoghurt and a sprinkle of pumpkin seeds.

VERY BERRY AND BEET SMOOTHIE

Serves 1–2
Prep time: 8–10 minutes
+ chilling time

This berry smoothie is my kind of mauve and the blackcurrants, blueberries and beetroot provide an abundance of antioxidants all in one go!

INGREDIENTS

150ml unsweetened apple juice

1 small cooked beetroot, peeled and sliced

1 medium pear, unpeeled, cored and chopped roughly

A handful of fresh or frozen blackcurrants (stalks removed if using fresh)

A handful of fresh blueberries

4 tablespoons unsweetened, plain soya or coconut yoghurt

½ tablespoon ground chia seeds

A pinch of ground cinnamon

A pinch of ground or freshly grated nutmeg

½ teaspoon maple syrup

Hulled hemp seeds

METHOD

Place all of the ingredients, except the hemp seeds, in a blender jug and blend until smooth. Pour into a large glass, or two smaller ones, and chill for about 15–20 minutes to allow the chia seeds to thicken the smoothie. Just before serving, sprinkle with a teaspoon of hulled hemp seeds.

YUMMY CHILLED CHIA SEED, FIG AND PECAN OATMEAL

Serves 2–4
Prep time: 10 minutes
(+ overnight soaking)

A variation on porridge, this dish is prepared the night before and served cold with delicious toppings. The chia seeds are a good source of protein, calcium and balanced Omega-6 and Omega-3 fats. Dried figs are also an excellent source of calcium, so give yourself a boost for breakfast!

INGREDIENTS

40g fine oatmeal

2 tablespoons ground chia seeds

300ml soya milk or other plant milk

2 teaspoons almond butter

2 dried figs, chopped quite finely

8 pecan nuts (about 15g), chopped quite finely

TO SERVE

1 medium pear, unpeeled, cored and sliced

1 medium eating apple, such as Braeburn, unpeeled, cored and sliced

A handful of dried cranberries

METHOD

In a medium bowl place the oatmeal and chia seeds and pour over the soya milk. Stir in the almond butter, the chopped figs and chopped pecans. Place in the fridge overnight. The chia seeds and oatmeal will absorb the milk and in the morning you will have a lovely thick creamy consistency.

When ready to serve, spoon the oatmeal into breakfast bowls and top with the chopped pear, apple and cranberries. Yum!

A word about . . . oatmeal

Oatmeal is the whole oat grain including the bran (minus the inedible outer husk) ground into a 'meal' and is a common part of Scottish cookery. It is also naturally vegan. Oatmeal comes in different varieties or 'cuts' – fine, medium, rough and pinhead – and has different textures. See Nichola Fletcher's *The Scottish Oats Bible* for the complete lowdown on oats.

ZINGY ALL-DAY BRUNCH BOWL

Serves 2
Prep time: 10 minutes
Cooking time: 2–3 minutes
dry-frying

Full of different textures – from soft avocado to crunchy apple and smooth cucumber – and contrasting flavours, including sweet grapes, zesty lime and aromatic mint, this bowl of loveliness is ideal for a fresh start to the day or for a quick, nutrient-packed lunch.

For breakfast I like to serve it with plain soya yoghurt or coconut yoghurt. For lunch it goes well on a bed of watercress with rye bread or with warm Bannocks (p. 115).

INGREDIENTS

10 green seedless grapes, quartered

10cm piece of cucumber, peeled and chopped roughly

1 medium eating apple, such as Braeburn, unpeeled, cored and chopped roughly

1 avocado, peeled, stone removed and flesh chopped roughly

Juice of ½ lime

10–12 mint leaves, chopped finely

25g pumpkin seeds

A drizzle of rapeseed oil or hemp seed oil

Salt and freshly ground black pepper

METHOD

In a medium bowl, place the grapes, cucumber, apple and avocado. Squeeze over the lime juice and scatter with chopped mint.

In a small frying pan dry-toast the pumpkin seeds until they start to pop. Remove from the heat and add to the bowl.

Next, drizzle over a little oil and season to taste with salt and black pepper.

Stir everything together gently with a spoon until the ingredients are well mixed and coated with oil and lime juice. Eat straightaway or the same day (chill until required).

SOUPS

CARROT AND OATMEAL (ORCADIAN OATMEAL) SOUP

Serves 4
Prep time: 20 minutes
Cooking time:
30–35 minutes

Carrots are a staple root vegetable in Scotland and their natural sweetness means they can be used in both savoury and sweet recipes. They are also a great source of beta-carotene (which is converted by the body into vitamin A). This recipe hails from Orkney and is thickened with heart-healthy oatmeal and chunky vegetables.

INGREDIENTS

3 tablespoons olive oil or rapeseed oil

1 medium onion, peeled and chopped finely

2 large leeks (about 400g), trimmed and chopped finely

4 medium carrots (about 300g), scrubbed or peeled, trimmed and grated

¼ large yellow swede, or 3–4 small white turnips (about 150g), peeled and grated

3 tablespoons vegan Calvados (or alternative, see p. 21)

50g medium oatmeal

1 litre vegan stock

500ml unsweetened oat milk or other unsweetened plant milk

Salt and freshly ground black pepper

A small bunch of coriander, chopped roughly

A handful of pumpkin seeds

METHOD

In a medium saucepan or heavy-bottomed pan, heat the oil on a medium heat. Add the onion, leeks, carrots, swede (or turnip) and sweat, stirring occasionally, for about 15 minutes. Stir in the Calvados and cook vigorously on medium-high heat until the liquid has evaporated (2–3 minutes).

Reduce the heat to medium, then mix in the oatmeal and cook for another minute, stirring.

Add the stock, bring to the boil, reduce the heat to medium-low and simmer until the vegetables are soft (around 15 minutes). Stir in the oat milk, season to taste, and bring the soup to serving temperature – do not allow the liquid to boil at this stage.

Ladle the soup into warm bowls, sprinkle over the chopped coriander and pumpkin seeds, and serve with Kale Crisps (p. 36) or granary bread.

'COCK A LEEKIE' SOUP

Serves 4
Prep time: 15 minutes
Cooking time: 30 minutes

'Cock a Leekie' is a traditional Scottish crofter's soup that would have been made with the produce grown and reared on the land, including, unfortunately, a fowl or chicken. My vegan version uses smoked tofu instead, although tempeh (see A word about . . . tempeh, p. 69) could also be substituted in this dish. This soup is simple to prepare, has lovely, delicate flavours and is packed with good things: tofu is calcium-rich, while prunes are a super source of vitamin K and also contain vitamin A, iron, potassium and fibre.

INGREDIENTS

3 medium leeks, trimmed and cut into approx. 2cm rounds (about 375g prepped)

1 medium onion, peeled and cut into quarters

6 cloves

2 bay leaves

1 teaspoon dried thyme, or 3 teaspoons fresh thyme, leaves picked and chopped finely

½ teaspoon dried rosemary or 1½ teaspoons fresh rosemary, leaves picked and chopped finely

1½ litres of vegan stock mixed with ½ teaspoon yeast extract/Marmite

200g smoked tofu (such as Taifun), cut into small cubes

100g dried, stoned prunes, whole

Salt and freshly ground black pepper

A small bunch of parsley, chopped finely

Flax seed oil or rapeseed oil

METHOD

In a large heavy-based saucepan with a lid place the leeks, onion, cloves, bay leaves, thyme and rosemary. Pour over the stock, bring to the boil and then reduce the heat and simmer, partially covered, for 25 minutes or until the leeks and onion are tender.

Remove the bay leaves and cloves carefully with a spoon.

Add the smoked tofu and prunes, season to taste with salt and black pepper, and simmer for a further 5 minutes.

Ladle the soup into warm bowls, sprinkle with chopped parsley and drizzle over a little flax seed or rapeseed oil. Serve with Pumpkin Seed and Oat Soda Bread (p. 121) or another of your favourites.

COURGETTE AND BROAD BEAN SOUP

Serves 4
Prep time: 20 minutes
Cooking time: 45 minutes

This is one of my favourite soups, especially when courgettes and broad beans are in season during the summer. If you haven't put them together before, you are in for a treat! You can also use frozen broad beans year-round.

INGREDIENTS

1 tablespoon rapeseed oil +
½ tablespoon olive oil

1 onion, peeled and chopped finely

1 celery stick, trimmed and chopped roughly

2 medium courgettes (about 300g), trimmed and chopped roughly

2 small potatoes, peeled and chopped roughly

150ml vegan vermouth (or alternative, see p. 21)

1 litre vegan stock

200g freshly podded or frozen broad beans

Salt and freshly ground black pepper

A small bunch of parsley, chopped finely

Omega seed mix

METHOD

In a medium, heavy-based pan with a lid, heat the oil on medium heat, add the onion, celery and courgettes and sweat, partially covered, until softened – about 8–10 minutes.

Add the potatoes and sweat for a further 4–5 minutes, stirring regularly.

Add the vermouth, raise the temperature and cook vigorously for about 3 minutes to allow the liquid to evaporate. Now add the stock, bring to the boil, reduce the heat, partially cover and simmer for around 25 minutes. Stir in the broad beans and cook for a further 4–5 minutes (if using frozen beans, bring back to simmering heat), then season to taste with salt and black pepper.

Serve the soup as it is, or blend with a hand-held blender until smooth or, if you prefer, leave in some chunky bits. Ladle the soup into warm bowls and sprinkle with the chopped parsley and the Omega seed mix. Serve with Herb Scones (p. 116) or sourdough bread.

'CULLEN SKINK'

Serves 4
Prep time: 15 minutes
Cooking time: 30 minutes

Traditionally, Cullen skink is made with finnan haddie (haddock cold-smoked with unseasoned wood and peat), potatoes, onions and milk. It is a thick soup, a speciality of Cullen in Moray in the north-east corner of Scotland. 'Skink', however, is an old Scots word which refers to the 'shin' of beef from which soup was sometimes made. My flavoursome, plant-based alternative uses artichokes instead of haddock, soya milk and cream in place of dairy milk and seaweed to create a taste of the sea.

INGREDIENTS

2 medium onions, peeled and chopped finely

250g floury potatoes (such as King Edward or Maris Piper), peeled and cut into small pieces

400ml unsweetened soya milk or other plant milk

6 or so twists of freshly ground black pepper

5g arame seaweed, rinsed, soaked in water for 10 minutes, rinsed again and chopped finely

1 teaspoon dried thyme or 3 teaspoons fresh thyme, leaves picked and chopped finely

1 tablespoon olive oil or rapeseed oil

½ teaspoon English mustard

100g artichoke hearts (drained, if tinned, and rinsed if in oil), sliced thinly

100ml soya cream or other vegan cream

A small bunch of chives, chopped finely

Hulled hemp seeds

METHOD

In a large saucepan, place the onion and potatoes and cover with the soya milk. Add the black pepper, seaweed and thyme. Bring to just below boiling point, then reduce the heat and simmer gently for around 30 minutes until the vegetables have softened.

Remove from the heat, stir in the oil and mustard, and mash to thicken the soup. Next, add the artichokes and cream, return the pan to a low-to-medium heat and simmer for 2–3 minutes, stirring regularly and making sure not to boil.

Check seasoning and adjust if liked (seaweed can be salty so you may not need extra seasoning). Ladle the soup into warm bowls and sprinkle with chopped chives and hemp seeds. I like to serve this soup with seeded bread.

A word about . . . seaweed

Seaweed has long been used in Scottish cookery, traditionally for flavouring broths. I have come across several recipes in old Scottish recipe books which use dulse, which is a dark pink or mauve algae. F. Marian McNeill includes a Hebridean recipe for seaweed soup in *The Scots Kitchen* (1929) as well as a dish using dulse from the island of Barra and a sea-moss jelly.

Seaweed is rich in vitamins A and C, as well as in trace elements including calcium, potassium, iodine and iron, all absorbed from the sea. Other seaweeds which are used in cooking include arame, kombu and wakame. All are high in iodine, so use sparingly.

Dried seaweed can generally be picked up in Asian supermarkets and well-stocked health-food shops, as well as online. Opt for organic seaweed where possible to ensure its quality.

HARICOT BEAN SOUP

Serves 4
Prep time: 15 minutes
Cooking time: 55 minutes

Traditional Scottish haricot bean soup is made by soaking and then boiling the haricot beans with bacon and vegetables and then adding milk. With a nod to the Auld Alliance between Scotland and France, my vegan version draws on a typical French *mirepoix* base of onion, carrot and celery. This is a thick and warming soup – ideal for a cold day.

INGREDIENTS

3 tablespoons olive oil or rapeseed oil

2 medium onions, peeled and chopped finely

4 medium carrots (about 300g), scrubbed or peeled, trimmed and chopped finely

2 celery sticks, trimmed and chopped finely

4 large cloves of garlic, peeled and crushed

120ml vegan vermouth (or alternative, see p. 21)

2 x 400g tins haricot beans (480g net weight)

1 litre vegan stock

1 teaspoon dried oregano, or 3 teaspoons fresh oregano, chopped finely

4 bay leaves

Salt and freshly ground black pepper

A splash of hot water, if needed

METHOD

In a large heavy-based saucepan, heat the oil on a medium heat, add the onion, carrots and celery, and sweat until softened. Add the garlic and cook for a minute, stirring. Pour in the vermouth and cook on a medium heat until all the liquid has evaporated (about 3–4 minutes).

Drain the haricot beans, retaining the bean water/aquafaba for another recipe (such as Scotch Mist, p. 192). Along with the stock, oregano and bay leaves add the beans to the pan, bring to the boil, reduce the heat and simmer, partially covered, for 40 minutes. Season with salt and black pepper. Remove and discard the bay leaves.

Add half the soup to a blender jug and blend until thick and creamy, then return to the pan and mix with the remaining soup. Alternatively, blend all of the soup if you prefer it to be smooth. Bring to serving temperature, adding a little hot water if needed to bring the soup to your preferred consistency.

Ladle the soup into warm bowls and serve with Bannocks (p. 115) or sourdough bread.

LEEK AND POTATO SOUP WITH WHITE BEANS

Serves 4–6
Prep time: 15 minutes
Cooking time: 45 minutes

It doesn't come more traditional in the Scottish kitchen than leek and potato soup! I have added chives, which provide an extra kick in the taste department, and haricot beans, both for protein and texture. You can blend all or half the soup or leave it chunky – any way is the right way!

INGREDIENTS

2 tablespoons olive oil or rapeseed oil

1 medium onion, peeled and chopped finely

4 leeks (about 500g), trimmed and sliced finely

2 medium potatoes (about 300g), peeled and cut into cubes

2 tablespoons fresh chives, chopped finely

100ml vegan vermouth (or alternative, see p. 21)

1 teaspoon English mustard

1 litre vegan stock

½ teaspoon celery seed

Freshly ground black pepper

1 x 400g tin haricot beans, drained (240g net weight)

METHOD

In a large heavy-bottomed saucepan with a lid heat the oil on medium heat, then add the onion and leeks and sweat until softened. Next add the potatoes and cook for 5 minutes, stirring often to avoid them sticking to the bottom of the pan.

Add in the chives, then the vermouth, and cook until the liquid has evaporated (about 4–5 minutes). Next, stir in the mustard.

Add the stock, celery seed and 4–5 twists of black pepper. Bring to the boil then reduce the heat and simmer, partially covered, for 30 minutes or until the potatoes are tender but not falling apart. Stir in the beans and cook for a further 10 minutes. Taste and season, if required.

Blend half the soup, or leave it unblended, bring to serving temperature and ladle into warm bowls. Pumpkin Seed and Oat Soda Bread (p. 121) goes really well with this soup.

A word about . . . leeks

Leeks are a super source of vitamin K, a very good source of vitamins B6 and C, along with vitamins A and E. They contain copper, folate, iron and manganese, as well as calcium, dietary fibre, magnesium and Omega-3 fatty acids.

A word about . . . prebiotics

Leeks, together with other plants from the Allium family, including garlic and onions, are an excellent source of what are known as prebiotics, which help maintain a healthy digestive system. Other prebiotics include asparagus, bananas, beans, lentils and whole grains.

LENTIL SOUP

Serves 6–8
Prep time: 20 minutes
Cooking time: 45 minutes

This is a thick, hearty and typically Scottish soup which I love making in autumn and winter. Although traditionally made using bacon, I substitute smoked paprika, which adds a subtle smokiness and a bit of a kick. Lentils are full of protein as well as copper, iron and phosphorus, fibre, folate and manganese; you could eat this as a main meal like a stew.

INGREDIENTS

6 medium carrots (about 450g), scrubbed or peeled, trimmed and sliced finely

1 medium potato, peeled and chopped finely

2 tablespoons olive oil or rapeseed oil

2 medium onions, peeled and chopped finely

1 medium leek, trimmed and chopped finely

3 cloves of garlic, peeled and crushed

3 tablespoons vegan brandy (or alternative, see p. 21)

¼ teaspoon dried turmeric

½–¾ teaspoon smoked paprika (depending on how hot and smoky you want your soup to be)

1.5 litres vegan stock

200g red lentils, well rinsed

3 bay leaves

Freshly ground black pepper

TO SERVE

A handful of poppy seeds and hemp seeds mixed together (about 15g of each)

METHOD

In a metal or bamboo steamer (or using a colander over a pan of steaming water), steam the carrots and potato for around 8–10 minutes until a knife passes easily through them. Meanwhile, heat the oil on a medium heat in a heavy-based pan, add the onion and leeks and sweat until softened – about 8–10 minutes. Add the garlic and cook for a minute, stirring.

Next add the steamed carrots and potato and cook for 8–10 minutes. Stir in the brandy and keep mixing until the liquid has evaporated – about 3 minutes. Then add the turmeric and the smoked paprika and mix in thoroughly.

Add the stock, lentils, bay leaves and a few twists of pepper. Bring to the boil, then reduce the heat and simmer, uncovered, for 25–30 minutes or until the lentils are cooked. If the soup seems too thick for you, add a little hot water.

Taste and adjust the seasoning, if needed. Remove the bay leaves with a spoon and discard them, then ladle the soup into warm bowls.

Scatter over the seed mix and serve with warm, crusty bread.

MUSHROOM SOUP

Serves 4
Prep time: 15 minutes
Cooking time: 35 minutes

This is one of my all-time-favourite soups because I love mushrooms! The addition of vegan cream makes it smooth and velvety, as well as intensely mushroomy.

INGREDIENTS

5g dried shiitake or dried wild mushrooms, chopped roughly (or snipped with scissors)

50ml warm water

1½ tablespoons olive oil or rapeseed oil

1 medium onion, peeled and chopped finely

2 cloves of garlic, peeled and crushed

250g chestnut mushrooms, chopped roughly

250g white cap mushrooms, chopped roughly

4 tablespoons vegan sherry

500ml vegan stock

2 teaspoons dried thyme, or 6 teaspoons fresh thyme, leaves picked and chopped finely

1½ teaspoons balsamic vinegar

Salt and freshly ground black pepper

150ml soya cream or oat cream

TO SERVE

A small bunch of parsley, chopped finely

A handful of pumpkin seeds

METHOD

In a small bowl, soak the dried mushrooms in the warm water for 10 minutes.

Meanwhile in a medium saucepan with a lid heat the oil on a medium heat, add the onion and sweat until softened. Next, add the garlic and cook for a minute, stirring. Add both the fresh and the rehydrated mushrooms (including any residual soaking water) and cook for 5 minutes. Pour in the sherry and simmer for another 3–4 minutes to allow the alcohol to evaporate.

Stir in the stock and the thyme. Bring to the boil, then reduce the heat and simmer, partially covered, for 15 minutes.

Remove from the heat and allow the soup to cool slightly before stirring in the balsamic vinegar and seasoning to taste. Blend until smooth, then return to the pan.

Add the cream and bring to serving temperature (do not allow to boil). Taste and season again – you may want a few further twists of pepper at this point. Add a splash of hot water if you want to thin the soup a little before serving.

Pour into warm bowls and sprinkle the chopped parsley and pumpkin seeds over the soup. This earthy soup goes particularly well with rye bread.

SCOTCH BROTH

Serves 4
Prep time: 15–20 minutes
Cooking time: 60 minutes

Quintessentially Scottish, this soup was traditionally made using meat, barley, root vegetables and pulses. According to Sue Lawrence in her book *Scots Cooking*, the meat and vegetables might be cooked in the broth and then removed and served separately as a second course. My vegan version uses split peas and red lentils alongside vegetables and barley, and makes for a hearty bowlful! Both my husband and his sister, Irene, say this soup tastes just like their mother used to make it and I am chuffed that it seems authentic! The soup is served with grated carrot – an addition remembered by Irene from childhood.

INGREDIENTS

2 tablespoons olive oil or rapeseed oil

1 large onion, peeled and chopped finely

1 celery stick, trimmed and chopped finely

2 medium carrots (about 150g), scrubbed or peeled, trimmed and chopped finely

½ a medium swede (neep), peeled and cut into cubes

100g dried yellow split peas

75g pearl barley

1.5 litres vegan stock

½ teaspoon dried rosemary, or 1½ teaspoons fresh rosemary, leaves picked and chopped finely

½ teaspoon dried thyme, or 1½ teaspoons fresh thyme, leaves picked and chopped finely

3 bay leaves

75g red lentils, well rinsed

Salt and freshly ground black pepper

TO SERVE

A small bunch of parsley, chopped finely

Some grated carrot

METHOD

In a large saucepan heat the oil on a medium heat, add the onion, celery, carrot and swede and sweat until softened. Then stir in the split peas and pearl barley.

Add the stock, rosemary, thyme and bay leaves, bring to the boil, then reduce the heat and simmer for 30 minutes. Now add the red lentils and continue to simmer until the vegetables and pulses are cooked through – another 25–30 minutes or so should do it.

Remove and discard the bay leaves, season to taste and pour into warm bowls. Sprinkle the chopped parsley and some grated carrot over the top and serve with Bannocks (p. 115) or sourdough bread.

SPICY PARSNIP SOUP

Serves 4
Prep time: 15 minutes
Cooking time: 60 minutes

Parsnips are wonderful, naturally sweet and earthy root vegetables which are in season in Scotland throughout the autumn and winter months. They are rich in fibre, vitamin C, folate and manganese, as well as being a good source of potassium. Adding a little spice rounds out the flavour of this soup.

INGREDIENTS

2 tablespoons olive oil or rapeseed oil

1 large onion, peeled and chopped finely

4 medium parsnips (about 650g), trimmed, peeled, and diced

1 medium potato, peeled and diced

1 teaspoon garam masala

1 teaspoon ground cumin

3 tablespoons vegan vermouth (or alternative, see p. 21)

1.5 litres vegan stock

100ml unsweetened soya milk or oat milk

Salt and freshly ground black pepper

Plain vegan yoghurt

Hulled hemp seeds

METHOD

In a large saucepan with a lid gently heat the oil on medium heat, add the onion and sweat until softened – about 10 minutes. Add the diced parsnip and potato and cook for a further 10 minutes, stirring regularly.

Stir in the garam masala and ground cumin and cook for 1 minute, stirring continuously. Then pour in the vermouth and cook for 2–3 minutes to allow the liquid to evaporate and lift the spices off the bottom of the pan.

Add the stock, bring to the boil, then reduce the heat and simmer partially covered, until the parsnips and potatoes are tender when tested with a knife: this may take 40–50 minutes.

Remove from the heat and blend the soup. Return to the pan, stir in the soya/oat milk, season to taste and heat through to serving temperature (do not allow to boil at this point). If the soup is a little too thick for your liking, add a little more milk.

Pour into warm bowls, add a swirl of yoghurt and a sprinkle of hulled hemp seeds, and serve with seeded bread.

SPLIT PEA SOUP

Serves 4
Prep time: 25 minutes
(+ overnight soaking)
Cooking time:
60–90 minutes (mostly
unattended)

This warming winter soup is traditionally made in Scotland with bacon, so my vegan alternative gets its rich earthy flavours from thyme, bay leaves and smoked paprika. Yellow split peas provide protein and are also an excellent source of fibre, iron, magnesium and vitamin B6.

The yellow split peas need to be put on to soak the day before you make this. They take a while to cook, but the soup is worth it if you have some time at the weekend and makes a super Sunday supper.

INGREDIENTS

1 tablespoon olive oil or rapeseed oil

1 medium leek, trimmed and chopped finely

1 large carrot, scrubbed or peeled, trimmed and grated

3 tablespoons vegan vermouth or apple juice

1 teaspoon dried thyme, or 3 teaspoons fresh thyme, leaves picked and chopped finely

¼ teaspoon smoked paprika

1 teaspoon freshly squeezed lemon juice

220g dried yellow split peas, rinsed, soaked in cold water for 12 hours and rinsed again

1.4 litres vegan stock

3 bay leaves

Salt and freshly ground black pepper

TO SERVE

A handful of sesame seeds

METHOD

In a large, heavy-based pan with a lid, heat the oil on a medium heat, add the leek and carrot and sweat until softened.

Add the vermouth or apple juice, thyme, paprika and lemon juice, increase the heat and cook for 1–2 minutes vigorously to allow the liquid to evaporate. Stir in the prepared yellow split peas and add the stock and bay leaves. Bring to the boil, then reduce the heat and simmer, covered, for around 60–90 minutes or until the split peas have softened.

Remove the bay leaves, and then blend the soup. Season to taste and then bring to serving temperature.

Ladle the soup into warm bowls and sprinkle some sesame seeds over the top. Serve with good crusty bread.

WATERCRESS SOUP

Serves 4
Prep time: 15 minutes
Cooking time: 30 minutes

This hearty soup includes not only earthy watercress but black-eyed beans, which add protein and fibre to the dish. To ensure the watercress is fresh, keep it in the fridge in a box with a lid and use within 48 hours.

INGREDIENTS

1 tablespoon olive oil or rapeseed oil

1 medium onion, peeled and chopped finely

1 medium potato, peeled and chopped roughly

1 bunch of watercress, chopped roughly

1 x 400g tin black-eyed beans, drained (net weight 240g), rinsed in cold water

1 litre vegan stock

½–¾ teaspoon ground nutmeg

Salt and freshly ground black pepper

METHOD

In a medium heavy-based saucepan with a lid heat the oil on a medium heat, add the onion and sweat until softened.

Next, add the potato, watercress and beans and cook for 2–3 minutes, stirring. Pour in the stock, bring to the boil, turn down the heat and simmer, partially covered, for 25 minutes or until the potato has softened (but has not fallen apart). Remove from the heat and blend until smooth.

Bring gently to serving temperature, stir in half a teaspoon of nutmeg and season to taste with salt and black pepper. Taste again and add in the remaining quarter teaspoon of nutmeg, if liked.

Pour into warm bowls and to serve scatter over a few Kale Crisps (p. 36) or sesame seeds. This soup pairs well with Herb Scones (p. 116).

A word about . . . watercress

Watercress is rich in nutrients: a dark-green leafy vegetable that is full of goodness. It provides a good helping of calcium, folate, iron, magnesium, potassium and zinc, as well as vitamins A and C, and a super boost of vitamin K.

SALADS

ASPARAGUS, FENNEL, AVOCADO AND ORANGE SALAD

Serves 4
Prep time: 10–15 minutes
Cooking time:
5 minutes (steaming)

This is a vibrant salad which combines several textures – the creaminess of avocado with the crispness of fennel – and different flavours: citrusy orange, aniseed notes of fennel and the earthy woodiness of asparagus. There is plenty of vitamin C in this salad, while the avocado provides vitamin K and folate too.

INGREDIENTS

12–14 asparagus stalks

100g mixed salad leaves

1 small fennel bulb

1 medium, ripe avocado

3 spring onions

1 medium orange

1 tablespoon sesame seeds

1 tablespoon hulled hemp seeds

Salt and freshly ground black pepper

Hemp seed oil or rapeseed oil

A handful of pistachio nuts

METHOD

Trim off the woody end of the asparagus spears, discard, then steam the asparagus for about 5 minutes. Rinse with cold water and set aside to cool and dry completely.

Scatter the salad leaves on a salad platter or large plate.

Trim and slice the fennel bulb very finely and arrange on the salad platter followed by the cooled asparagus.

Cut the avocado in half and remove the stone carefully. Peel, cut the flesh into thin slices and add to the salad.

Trim and slice the spring onions and arrange on the platter. Then peel the orange, cut into segments over a bowl and place the segments on top of the salad. Set aside any juice left in the bowl.

Sprinkle over the sesame seeds and the hemp seeds and then season with salt and black pepper. Finish with a good drizzle of oil, spoon over the reserved orange juice and scatter over the pistachios.

BEETROOT SALAD WITH VEGAN CROWDIE

Serves 2
Prep time: 10 minutes
(+ overnight preparation
of the crowdie)

Beets take centre stage in this salad, alongside my vegan version of crowdie, a soft and slightly soured Scottish cheese traditionally made by crofters and said to have been introduced to Scotland by the Vikings! The crowdie needs to be prepared in advance – see the page opposite for the recipe.

INGREDIENTS FOR THE BEETROOT SALAD

100g watercress

3 medium cooked beetroot (if using shop-bought, without vinegar)

1 small red onion or 3 salad onions

25g hazelnuts

50g vegan crowdie (recipe follows)

Salt and freshly ground black pepper

A small handful of fresh dill, chopped finely to make about a tablespoon

INGREDIENTS FOR THE DRESSING

½ tablespoon hazelnut oil. (or other oil)

1 tablespoon freshly squeezed orange juice

¼ teaspoon apple cider vinegar

METHOD

Arrange the watercress on a serving plate. Cut the beetroot into wedges and arrange on top of the watercress. Peel the onion (or trim, if using salad onions), chop finely and scatter over the top of the beetroot. Chop the hazelnuts finely and sprinkle them over the salad too. Then, with a spoon, dot small pieces of the crowdie over the salad and season everything well with salt and black pepper.

In a small jug or cup, mix the oil with the orange juice and apple cider vinegar, and spoon the dressing over the salad. Then sprinkle the dill over the dish.

If you have used fresh beetroot and retained the beet tops, prepare them according to the instructions in the box opposite and serve on the side.

This salad goes well with Pumpkin Seed and Oat Soda Bread (p. 121) or toasted sourdough.

A word about . . . beetroot

Beetroot is a splendid Scottish root vegetable for its colour (usually a deep, gorgeous crimson red), its earthy flavour and its versatility: it can be used both raw and cooked and in both sweet and savoury dishes. It contains folates, as well as the B vitamins niacin, pantothenic acid and pyridoxine, and minerals such as copper, iron, magnesium and manganese.

VEGAN CROWDIE

INGREDIENTS

3 tablespoons plain unsweetened
soya yoghurt

METHOD

To make this soft cheese spoon the yoghurt into a piece of clean muslin
over a bowl, tie tightly with string and hang from the handle of a kitchen
cupboard over the bowl overnight.

In the morning, discard the strained liquid from the bowl and place the
curds or 'crowdie' from the muslin in the bowl and refrigerate until needed.

It will keep for a day or two in the fridge. Crowdie can also be served with
oatcakes for a satisfying snack!

Preparing fresh beetroot

Wash the beets thoroughly and top and tail them. Discard the tails, but
retain the usable beetroot tops (which should be bright purple, if fresh).
Dry with a paper towel and set aside. Place the beets in a medium-large
saucepan with a lid, cover with cold water, bring to the boil and boil hard
for 5 minutes, then reduce the heat and simmer for 1½ hours, covered,
until cooked. Discard the water, cool the beets until they can be safely
handled and then peel them carefully.

To prepare beet tops, in a small frying pan add a little rapeseed oil
and bring to a medium-high heat. Add the beet tops and sauté for 6–8
minutes. Season with salt and freshly ground pepper before serving.

BROAD BEAN AND BLACKBERRY SALAD

Serves 2–4
Prep time: 15 minutes
Cooking time: 5–6 minutes

This fresh and vibrant salad is ideal for late summer when blackberries and broad beans are in season. I use rapeseed oil in the dressing, which gives the salad a lovely buttery golden hue.

INGREDIENTS

125g freshly podded (or frozen) broad beans

1 large courgette

30g alfalfa sprouts

3 salad onions

100g blackberries

25g pumpkin seeds

Salad cress or pea shoots (optional)

Salt and freshly ground black pepper

INGREDIENTS FOR THE DRESSING

3 tablespoons rapeseed oil

2 tablespoons apple juice

2 teaspoons apple cider vinegar

1 teaspoon vegan honey or coconut nectar

Salt and freshly ground black pepper

METHOD

Place the broad beans in a medium saucepan and cover with cold water. Bring to the boil, then reduce the heat and simmer for 5–6 minutes. If using frozen beans, cook for 3–4 minutes. Drain, rinse in cold water and set aside.

Trim the courgette and peel it into large strips, lengthways, down to the seeds (reserve the remaining courgette for soup), then arrange it on a large plate or platter.

Add the alfalfa sprouts.

Trim and slice the salad onions and add to the plate, then add the broad beans.

Cut the blackberries in half and add them to the salad.

Sprinkle the pumpkin seeds and salad cress (or pea shoots, if using) over the salad and season well with salt and black pepper.

To make the dressing, combine all of the ingredients in a jam jar with a lid and shake well (with the lid on!) to mix. Drizzle over the salad before serving with freshly made Bannocks (p. 115) or your favourite bread. I like to serve this with Herb Scones (p. 116).

BUCKWHEAT, CARROT AND APPLE SALAD

Serves 4–6
Prep time: 20 minutes
Cooking time: 8–10 minutes

This healthy salad provides protein as well as an array of vitamins and minerals. It has a lovely nutty texture from the buckwheat and other seeds, natural sweetness from the carrots and apricots, a zinginess from the apple and lemon, and a decisive crunch from the celery and nuts.

INGREDIENTS

200g buckwheat

300ml water

3 medium carrots

40g walnuts

25g sesame seeds

25g hulled hemp seeds

2 dessert apples

2 teaspoons freshly squeezed lemon juice

3 celery sticks

2 spring onions

4 dried, unsulphured apricots

45g raisins

3 tablespoons olive oil or rapeseed oil

6 tablespoons apple juice

Salt and freshly ground black pepper

A small bunch of parsley

METHOD

Rinse the buckwheat thoroughly and then place it in a medium saucepan with a lid. Cover with the water and bring to the boil. Reduce the heat to a simmer and cook for 7–8 minutes, covered. Stir frequently in the final minutes of cooking to avoid the buckwheat sticking to the bottom of the pan. Remove from the heat, rinse in cold water and set aside to cool completely.

While the buckwheat is cooking initially, scrub or peel, trim and then grate the carrots into a salad bowl.

Roughly chop the walnuts and add them with the sesame seeds and hemp seeds to the bowl.

Core and roughly chop the apples, unpeeled, and add them to the bowl. Then spoon the lemon juice over the apples.

Trim and chop the celery finely and add to the bowl.

Next, trim and thinly slice the onions and chop the apricots finely and add them with the raisins to the other ingredients.

Now add the prepared buckwheat and then the oil and apple juice. Mix thoroughly with salad servers and season well with salt and black pepper. Finally, chop the parsley and sprinkle over the salad. Chill until ready to serve. This will keep for a day or two in the fridge, covered.

A word about . . . buckwheat

Buckwheat is actually a seed rather than a grain. Contrary to its name, it contains no wheat and is suitable for use in a gluten-free diet. It is a good source of protein and magnesium.

EASY WATERCRESS SALAD

Serves 2
Prep time: 10 minutes
Cooking time: 4–5 minutes

This simple, light and easy-to-make five-ingredient salad contains calcium and iron from the watercress, protein from the peas, iron from the sun-dried tomatoes, vitamin C from the orange (which helps with iron absorption) and protein, copper, magnesium, manganese and zinc from the pumpkin seeds. It is colourful and pretty tasty too!

INGREDIENTS

100g watercress

200g frozen garden peas

25g sun-dried tomatoes

1 medium orange

40g pumpkin seeds

Salt and freshly ground black pepper

Hemp seed oil or rapeseed oil, to serve

A squeeze of fresh lemon, to serve

METHOD

Trim, roughly chop and add the watercress to a medium salad bowl.

Place the peas in a small pan, cover with water, bring to the boil and cook for 2–3 minutes. Drain, rinse in cold water, pat dry and then add to the salad.

Chop the sun-dried tomatoes finely and add them to the bowl. Next, peel and cut the orange into segments (discarding the pith and pips) and add to the salad, together with any juice you can capture from the orange.

Place the pumpkin seeds in a small frying pan on low to medium heat and gently dry-fry them until they start to colour and pop. Sprinkle over the salad.

Season to taste with salt and freshly ground black pepper, then drizzle with oil and a squeeze of lemon.

Serve for lunch with slices of smoked tofu or as a side salad to a main dish.

KALE, CHICKPEA, CRANBERRY AND SESAME SALAD

Serves 2–4
Prep time: 10 minutes
Cooking time: 4–5 minutes

These ingredients go beautifully together, colour-wise, flavour-wise and health-wise. The cranberries are the jewels in this salad and pack in vitamin C, E and K, as well as manganese, while the chickpeas provide protein and the sesame seeds calcium, iron, magnesium and phosphorous, as well as copper and manganese. Kale has never tasted so good!

INGREDIENTS

125g kale

1 x 400g tin chickpeas. (240g net weight)

2 celery sticks

40g dried cranberries

20g sesame seeds

25g pumpkin seeds

2 tablespoons hulled hemp seeds

A small bunch of parsley

Salt and freshly ground black pepper

INGREDIENTS FOR THE DRESSING

3 tablespoons rapeseed oil

1 teaspoon freshly squeezed lemon juice

½ teaspoon garlic granules

METHOD

Remove the thick stalks from the kale and discard them, then steam the kale for 4–5 minutes in a steamer. Rinse in cold water, pat dry and add to a large salad bowl. Drain the chickpeas, reserving the liquid for another recipe that uses aquafaba/bean water (such as Scotch Mist, p. 192) and add to the bowl.

Trim and slice the celery finely and add it to the bowl. Then roughly chop the cranberries and add them to the bowl together with the sesame seeds, pumpkin seeds and hemp seeds. Chop the parsley finely and add it to the salad, then season with salt and black pepper. Chill until needed.

Just before serving, in a small bowl mix together the oil, lemon juice and garlic granules. Drizzle the dressing over the salad and mix everything together.

This salad pairs well with seeded wholemeal bread or Oatcakes (p. 118).

QUICK PICKLED 'HERRINGS'

Serves 4
Prep time: 15 minutes
Cooking time: 30 minutes

'Soused' herrings were a traditional food in Scotland and provided a good way to preserve the catch. My vegan alternative uses celeriac, which is rich in vitamin K, some essential minerals such as phosphorus, iron, calcium, copper and manganese, and some of the B-complex vitamins and vitamin C.

Mushrooms are the only plant source of vitamin D and are also a good source of fibre, protein and a range of vitamins and minerals. Pumpkin seeds and sesame seeds are an excellent source of tryptophan. The addition of seaweed and seeds rounds out the nutritional profile of this nourishing and tasty dish.

INGREDIENTS

7g arame seaweed

½ a medium celeriac

100g button mushrooms

1 medium onion, peeled and sliced finely

2 bay leaves

½ teaspoon pink peppercorns + ½ teaspoon black peppercorns (or 1 teaspoon of black peppercorns)

1 teaspoon allspice berries

1 teaspoon soft brown sugar

200ml hot water

2 tablespoons apple cider vinegar

25g pumpkin seeds

20g sesame seeds

METHOD

Preheat the oven to 160°C.

Rinse the seaweed, soak for 10 minutes in cold water and rinse again. Peel and quarter the celeriac and cut into thin slices. Slice the mushrooms, and peel and slice the onion finely.

Place the seaweed, celeriac and mushrooms in a shallow 24cm square ovenproof dish and cover with the sliced onions.

Add the bay leaves and scatter over the peppercorns and allspice berries.

In a small bowl or jug, dissolve the sugar in the hot water. Stir in the apple cider vinegar, then pour the liquid over the vegetables. Cover the dish with foil and cook for 30 minutes in the preheated oven.

Remove from the oven and cool before sprinkling with the pumpkin seeds and sesame seeds. I like to serve this dish with a green salad and rye bread. This will keep in the fridge for a couple of days.

RAW SLAW DELUXE

Serves 4
Prep time: 20 minutes
Cooking time: 5–6 minutes

This is a rather luxurious coleslaw! To Scottish-grown carrots, cabbage, apple and radishes, I add broad beans, sesame seeds, pumpkin seeds and poppy seeds, as well as raisins. There is protein, iron, calcium and an array of vitamins and minerals in this super slaw.

While the slaw makes a light salad for lunch or brunch, it is also a lovely crunchy accompaniment to vegan burgers, vegetable bakes and vegan haggis.

INGREDIENTS

75g freshly podded (or frozen) broad beans

1 dessert apple

Juice of ½ a freshly squeezed lemon

3–4 carrots

¼ of a white or red cabbage

4 radishes

75g raisins

25g sesame seeds

25g pumpkin seeds

1 tablespoon poppy seeds

4 tablespoons olive oil or rapeseed oil

Salt and freshly ground black pepper

METHOD

Cook the broad beans in boiling water for 5–6 minutes if freshly podded, or 3–4 minutes if frozen. Drain, rinse in cold water, pat dry and add the beans to a medium salad bowl.

Core and quarter the apple and grate it into the bowl, then sprinkle the lemon juice on top. Peel or scrub, trim and grate the carrots into the bowl. Trim and shred the cabbage roughly and add to the bowl. Slice the radishes finely and place in the bowl. Then stir in the raisins.

Toast the sesame seeds and pumpkin seeds in a dry frying pan on low heat until the sesame seeds start to release a lovely aroma and the pumpkin seeds start to pop (about 5–6 minutes). Cool a little, then add to the salad with the poppy seeds. Stir in the oil, season with salt and black pepper, then mix everything together well with salad servers. Chill until required.

This keeps in the fridge, covered, for a couple of days.

SUPER SALAD

Serves 4
Prep time: 20 minutes
Cooking time: 5–6 minutes

If, like me, you have been giving some thought to how to pack more calcium into your plant-based diet, here's a one-bowl super salad that goes a long way to providing your six to eight servings of calcium-rich foods per day! Ideally, have some of this for lunch and for supper or across a couple of days, as calcium is best consumed at different meals. Combined with vitamin D-providing mushrooms, vitamin C-providing orange and parsley, and with protein and iron from the black-eyed beans, this is a healthy and inviting bowl of goodness.

INGREDIENTS

1 small head of broccoli

100g mushrooms

3 medium carrots

1 x 400g tin black-eyed beans, drained (240g, net weight), rinsed in cold water

30g almonds

1 large orange

2 dried figs

2 tablespoons sesame seeds

Salt and freshly ground black pepper

A small bunch of parsley

A squeeze of fresh lemon

3 tablespoons rapeseed oil

METHOD

Cut the broccoli into small florets and the mushrooms into quarters. Steam together for 5–6 minutes (the broccoli should still have some bite) and then run under a cold tap to cool. Set aside to cool and dry completely.

While the broccoli and mushrooms are steaming, peel, trim and grate the carrots and place them in a large salad bowl together with the black-eyed beans and the almonds.

Peel the orange, cut it into segments (removing and discarding the pith and pips) and add them to the salad bowl. Squeeze over any remaining juice from what is left of the orange. Chop the figs and add them with the sesame seeds to the bowl. Next add the cooled broccoli and mushrooms.

Season well with salt and black pepper and, just before serving, chop the parsley roughly (to make 2–3 tablespoons) and scatter it over the salad. Add a good squeeze of lemon, spoon over the oil and mix the salad together with salad servers.

Pile into bowls and serve with thick granary bread or oatcakes. This keeps in the fridge for 2–3 days.

BREAD
AND ACCOMPANIMENTS

BANANA, DATE AND PECAN LOAF WITH CHOCOLATE CHIPS

Makes 1 loaf
Prep time: 15 minutes
Cooking time: 70 minutes
(mostly unattended)

This is a teatime – or anytime – treat which is sweetened with bananas, dates, coconut sugar and blackstrap molasses. With very little oil needed, this loaf is a relatively guilt-free pleasure.

INGREDIENTS

4 ripe bananas, peeled

2 tablespoons plain, unsweetened soya yoghurt or other vegan alternative

2 tablespoons olive oil, rapeseed oil or organic sunflower oil

1 flax seed egg (1 tablespoon ground flax seeds mixed with 3 tablespoons cold water and set aside for 5 minutes to thicken)

6 tablespoons coconut sugar

1 tablespoon blackstrap molasses

225g wholemeal self-raising flour

2 heaped teaspoons baking powder

4 pitted Medjool dates, or other soft dates, chopped into small pieces

30g pecans, chopped roughly

50g vegan dark chocolate chips

METHOD

Preheat the oven to 180°C. Line a 23cm x 13cm baking tin with baking parchment.

In a large mixing bowl, mash the bananas with a potato masher or fork. Add the yoghurt, oil, flax seed egg, coconut sugar and blackstrap molasses and mix together well.

Sift in the flour and baking powder, and stir gently until well combined.

Carefully stir in the dates, pecans and chocolate chips. The batter will be quite thick; this is how it should be.

Scoop the batter into the prepared baking tin and spread it evenly with a spatula.

Bake in the preheated oven for 45 minutes, uncovered, and then cover with baking parchment and cook for a further 25 minutes. The cake is cooked when a skewer inserted into the middle of the cake comes out clean.

Remove from the oven and cool for 30 minutes in the tin before tipping out onto a wire rack. Peel off the baking parchment and cool completely before cutting into slices. This will keep for 3–4 days in an airtight tin.

BANNOCKS

Makes 4 bannocks
Prep time: 15 minutes
Cooking time: 20 minutes

A bannock is unleavened bread traditionally made from oatmeal or beremeal.

Bannocks are very quick and simple to make, as there is no proving or kneading time required. They also look rather rustic. If you cannot find beremeal, oatmeal can be used instead.

INGREDIENTS

50ml unsweetened plain soya milk or other plant milk

1 teaspoon apple cider vinegar

125g beremeal (or medium oatmeal)

125g organic wholemeal self-raising flour

½ teaspoon bicarbonate of soda

½ teaspoon salt

½ teaspoon dark muscovado sugar

25ml olive oil or rapeseed oil

50ml plain soya yoghurt or other vegan alternative

Cold water, as needed

METHOD

Preheat the oven to 180°C. Lightly dust a baking tray with flour.

In a small jug or bowl measure out the soya milk and then add the vinegar. Set aside for 5 minutes to allow the mixture to curdle.

Meanwhile, in a large bowl, mix together the beremeal (or oatmeal, if using), wholemeal flour, bicarbonate of soda, salt and sugar.

Add the oil and rub it into the flour. Next, add the curdled soya milk and soya yoghurt and bring the mixture together with your hands into a soft dough. If using beremeal, you might need to add a splash or two of cold water to bring the dough together.

Remove the dough from the bowl and with the edge of your palm press it into a rough circle of around ½cm thick (the dough may splay out at the edges, which is fine). Cut the dough into four large triangles and place them on the baking tray.

Bake in the oven for 10 minutes, turn, and bake for a further 10 minutes until golden brown.

Remove from the oven and transfer to a wire baking rack to cool. These are best eaten on the same day they are made. I like to make them first thing in the morning in time for lunch!

A word about . . . beremeal

Beremeal is a wholegrain flour made from bere, a variety of barley dating back to the Bronze Age, which is still grown in the far north of Scotland. It adds a nutty taste and texture to bannocks and other baked goods.

There are two mills in Scotland currently making traditional beremeal: Golspie Mill in Sutherland and Barony Mill on Birsay on the Orkney Islands.

Beremeal can be found in health-food shops and in various outlets around the UK.

HERB SCONES

Makes 6–7 small scones
Prep time: 10 minutes
Cooking time:
10–12 minutes

These herby scones go well with soups and salads and are especially delicious when just baked and served warm.

INGREDIENTS

120ml unsweetened plain soya milk or other plant milk

1 teaspoon apple cider vinegar

240g organic wholemeal self-raising flour (or 120g wholemeal and 120g organic white self-raising flour)

¼ teaspoon salt

½ teaspoon dried oregano, or 1½ teaspoons fresh oregano, chopped finely

½ teaspoon dried rosemary, or 1½ teaspoons fresh rosemary, leaves picked and chopped finely

½ teaspoon dried thyme, or 1½ teaspoons fresh thyme, leaves picked and chopped finely

3 tablespoons olive oil or rapeseed oil

Soya milk to glaze

METHOD

Preheat the oven to 220°C. Lightly dust a medium baking tray with flour.

In a small jug or bowl mix together the soya milk and the apple cider vinegar and set aside for 5 minutes or so to allow the mixture to curdle.

Into a medium mixing bowl sieve the flour, then add the salt.

In a pestle and mortar, grind the oregano, rosemary and thyme and mix in thoroughly with the flour.

Add the oil and rub it into the flour mixture with your fingertips until it resembles fine breadcrumbs. Stir in the curdled milk and bring the mixture together with your hands to form a soft dough.

Empty the dough out onto a floured surface and gently press it with your hands to enlarge it into a thick round circle from which you can cut out 4 scones with a small round biscuit cutter. Bring the remaining dough back together, press it out again and cut out 2 (or 3) further scones.

Place the scones on the baking sheet, dab the tops with soya milk and bake in the oven for 10–12 minutes or until golden brown.

MORNING ROLLS

Makes 8 rolls
Prep time: 20 minutes
(+ 30 minutes proving time)
Cooking time:
20–22 minutes

Scottish morning rolls or floury baps are traditionally soft and white. My recipe uses wholemeal bread flour, as I think it produces a better taste and texture, as well as providing some health benefits from the inclusion of the bran. This is a roll which goes particularly well with a vegan sausage or vegan 'burger' and all the trimmings. Or add your favourite sandwich filling and lots of salad leaves for a delicious lunch.

INGREDIENTS

250g stoneground strong wholemeal bread flour

250g unbleached strong white bread flour

1 teaspoon salt

1 x 7g packet of easy-bake dried yeast

Around 290ml tepid water

Olive oil or rapeseed oil

METHOD

Sprinkle a baking tray with flour and set aside.

In a large bowl mix together the two types of flour and salt. Then stir in the yeast. Gradually add as much of the water as you need to bring the flour mixture together with your hands to form a dough which is soft and not sticky. Place the dough on a floured board or surface and knead for 7 minutes or so, ending with a rounded loaf-shape.

Put the dough back in the mixing bowl, rub the surface with a little oil and cover the bowl with a clean tea towel. Leave to rise somewhere warm for 30 minutes.

After about 20 minutes, preheat the oven to 230°C.

When it is ready, knead the dough again for a few minutes and then divide it into eight equal pieces. With floured hands shape each piece of dough into rolls and place on the baking tray.

Bake in the oven for 20–22 minutes, adding a splash of water to the oven as you close the oven door to help give the rolls a crust. The rolls are done if they sound hollow when tapped on the base. Remove from the oven and place on a wire baking rack to cool.

OATCAKES

Makes around 14 medium
oatcakes
Prep time: 15 minutes
Cooking time:
30–35 minutes

Oatcakes are the classic Scottish savoury biscuit and are made with heart-healthy oatmeal and oats. They vary in thickness and shape according to region, and traditionally were cooked on an iron 'girdle' (a griddle) placed over the fire. My oatcakes are cooked in the oven and are round and crunchy medium oatcakes rather than thin, crispy, thick, rough or triangular ones!

These are quick to make and bake. You can experiment by adding dried herbs (oregano, rosemary or thyme) to the mix to vary the taste or by using fine or coarse oatmeal to vary the texture. I like mine with sesame seeds mixed in.

INGREDIENTS

150g fine or medium oatmeal

25g rolled oats

100g organic wholemeal spelt flour

2 tablespoon sesame seeds

¾ teaspoon salt

2 tablespoons olive oil or rapeseed oil

70ml hot water

1 flax seed egg (1 tablespoon ground flax seeds mixed with 3 tablespoons cold water and set aside for a few minutes to thicken)

Extra flour for rolling out the oatcakes

METHOD

Preheat the oven to 180°C. Lightly dust a large baking tray with flour.

In a large mixing bowl, place the oatmeal, oats, flour, sesame seeds and salt and mix together. Make a well in the centre of the flour mix, pour in the oil and hot water and stir until combined. Then stir in the flax seed egg. With floured hands, bring the mixture together into a ball.

Tip the dough out onto a floured board and roll out to around half a centimetre thickness. Cut out into rounds using a medium biscuit or cookie cutter. Gather the offcuts of dough, and re-roll and cut out until you have used it all.

Place the oatcakes on the prepared baking sheet and bake for around 30 minutes. Cool on a wire rack before serving.

PUMPKIN SEED AND OAT SODA BREAD

Makes 1 loaf
Prep time: 15 minutes
Cooking time:
35–40 minutes

Soda bread is made without yeast and doesn't require kneading, proving or knocking back. It uses vegan buttermilk (soured soya milk) and the result is a loaf which is almost scone-like. I like using spelt flour for its flavour and texture and adding oats and pumpkin seeds to the mix for an extra protein boost, although you could use other seeds, such as sunflower or sesame, if you like.

INGREDIENTS

275ml soya milk

1 teaspoon apple cider vinegar

225g unbleached strong white bread flour

225g wholemeal spelt flour

50g rolled oats

1 teaspoon salt

1 teaspoon bicarbonate of soda

½ teaspoon muscovado or soft brown sugar

25ml olive oil or rapeseed oil

50g pumpkin seeds

METHOD

Preheat the oven to 200°C. Lightly dust a medium baking sheet with flour.

In a small jug, combine the soya milk and apple cider vinegar and set aside for 5 minutes or so to curdle.

In a large bowl mix together the two types of flour, oats, salt, bicarbonate of soda and sugar. Add the oil and rub it into the flour with your fingertips until the mixture resembles fine breadcrumbs, then stir in the pumpkin seeds.

Next add as much of the curdled soya milk as you need to bring the mixture together with your hands to form a soft (but not wet) dough.

On a floured surface with floured hands mould the dough into a rounded loaf.

Place the dough on the baking sheet and lightly score a large cross on its surface (this allows the dough to separate slightly and cook evenly).

Transfer to the oven, throw in a splash of water (which will help the bread to form a crust) and bake for 35–40 minutes.

To test whether the bread is cooked, remove it from the oven and tap the base, which should sound hollow. Place on a wire baking rack to cool. Best eaten on the day it is made or warmed in the oven if kept for a day or two.

MAINS

BRAISED CELERIAC AND HARICOT BEANS WITH HAZELNUT CRUST

Serves 4
Prep time: 15–20 minutes
Cooking time: 50 minutes

This is a super dish for autumn, rich and earthy with a soft texture from the celeriac and a crunchy topping. It is the ultimate comfort food. It is also full of protein from the beans and nuts, while the sun-dried tomatoes provide iron and other minerals as well as vitamins C and K.

INGREDIENTS FOR THE BRAISED CELERIAC AND HARICOT BEANS

½ medium celeriac, peeled and chopped into small chunks

1 small head of fennel, trimmed and sliced

400ml vegan stock

35g sun-dried tomatoes, chopped quite finely

1 tablespoon tomato paste

8–10 fresh sage leaves

A pinch of muscovado sugar

½ teaspoon freshly squeezed lemon juice

1 x 400g tin haricot beans (240g net weight), or other white beans such as butter beans

Salt and freshly ground black pepper

INGREDIENTS FOR THE HAZELNUT CRUST

2 tablespoons olive oil or rapeseed oil

75g rolled oats

50g medium oatmeal

30g hazelnuts, chopped finely

1 teaspoon dried oregano or 3 teaspoons fresh oregano, chopped finely

Salt and freshly ground black pepper

METHOD

Preheat the oven to 190°C.

Place the celeriac and fennel in a large saucepan and cover with the stock. Bring to the boil, reduce the heat and simmer for 20 minutes, uncovered, or until the celeriac and fennel are tender and the liquid has reduced.

While the vegetables are simmering, make the crust. In a medium saucepan, on medium heat, gently warm the oil. Add the oats, oatmeal and hazelnuts and stir together. Cook for 3–4 minutes, then stir in the oregano and cook for a further minute. Season to taste and set aside.

Return to the filling. Once the celeriac and fennel are cooked, stir in the sun-dried tomatoes, tomato paste, sage, sugar, lemon juice and haricot beans and cook for a further 8–10 minutes, adding a little water if necessary. Season to taste.

Transfer to an ovenproof pie dish, top with the crust mixture and bake in the oven for 18–20 minutes or until the crust is crunchy and golden brown.

Serve with steamed dark-green leafy vegetables.

CARROT, LEEK AND BUTTER BEAN CASSEROLE

Serves 4–6
Prep time: 15 minutes
Cooking time: 65 minutes

Carrots and leeks go beautifully together in this dish. The addition of butter beans adds protein and creaminess, which is accentuated with flavours of sage and bay leaves. This is one of my 'go to' autumn and winter warmers and a crowd pleaser for vegans and non-vegans alike.

INGREDIENTS

3 tablespoons olive oil or rapeseed oil

1 large onion, peeled and chopped finely

4 cloves of garlic, peeled and crushed

1 celery stick, trimmed and chopped finely

2 medium leeks, trimmed and chopped finely (about 250g prepped)

8 medium carrots (about 600g), peeled or scrubbed and sliced quite thinly in rounds

100ml vegan vermouth (or alternative, see p. 21)

1 teaspoon English mustard

2 x 400g tin butter beans (480g net weight)

2 tablespoons tomato purée dissolved in 4 tablespoons hot water

750ml vegan stock

1 tablespoon wholemeal flour mixed to a paste with 2 tablespoons cold water

3 bay leaves

Fresh sage leaves (15 or so)

Salt and freshly ground black pepper

METHOD

Preheat the oven to 160°C.

Bring the oil to a medium heat in a large saucepan. Add the onion, garlic, celery, leeks and carrots and sweat for around 15 minutes until softened.

Next stir in the vermouth and the mustard, and cook until the liquid has evaporated (about 3 minutes).

Drain the butter beans, saving the aquafaba/bean water to use in another recipe (see Scotch Mist, p. 192) and rinse in cold water. Add to the saucepan, along with the tomato purée and stock. Next add the flour paste and stir well. Sprinkle in the bay leaves and sage leaves, and season to taste.

Transfer to an ovenproof casserole dish and cook in the preheated oven for 45 minutes. After cooking, taste again and adjust the seasoning if needed. Remove the bay leaves before serving but leave in the cooked sage leaves.

Serve with Bannocks (p. 115) and green beans, Herb Scones (p. 116) or baked potatoes and garden peas.

'FISH' PIE WITH WATERCRESS SAUCE

Serves 4
Prep time: 20 minutes
Cooking time:
50–55 minutes

Fish pie is a popular Scottish dish, topped with mashed potato. My plant-based adaptation brings together celeriac, leek, artichoke and seaweed for a satisfyingly filling dish packed with vegetable goodness. The accompanying watercress sauce is rich in calcium, magnesium and potassium, as well as vitamins A, C and K.

INGREDIENTS FOR THE FILLING

8g arame seaweed

½ celeriac (or a small squash if you cannot get hold of celeriac), peeled and chopped into small pieces

2 medium leeks, trimmed and sliced finely (about 250g prepped)

1 celery stick, trimmed and sliced finely

2 artichoke hearts (from a tin or jar; drain first), chopped roughly

1½ tablespoons miso

2 tablespoons nutritional yeast flakes

½ teaspoon freshly squeezed lemon juice

400ml vegan stock

1 tablespoon chickpea (gram) flour

100ml unsweetened soya milk or other plant milk

Salt and freshly ground black pepper

INGREDIENTS FOR THE TOPPING

800g floury potatoes, peeled and quartered

1 tablespoon olive oil

100ml soya milk

Salt and freshly ground pepper

METHOD

Preheat the oven to 190°C.

Rinse the arame seaweed, soak in cold water for 10 minutes, rinse again and chop finely.

Meanwhile, in a large saucepan place all of the filling ingredients (except the chickpea flour and plant milk) and braise (i.e. cook in the juices), uncovered, for 25–30 minutes, stirring occasionally, or until the celeriac is cooked through. Add a splash of hot water if needed to keep the mixture moving.

While the filling is cooking make the potato topping. Bring the potatoes to the boil, then reduce the heat and simmer, partially covered, for 12–15 minutes. Drain, then add the oil and milk, mash and season to taste. Next, make the Watercress Sauce (recipe follows).

Keep an eye on the filling, and after 30 minutes, place the chickpea flour and 2 tablespoons of the measured soya milk into a small cup and mix to a paste. Add the remainder of the soya milk to the large pan of braised vegetables, bring to just below the boil, then remove from the heat and stir in the paste. Return to the heat immediately and cook, stirring regularly, for another 2–3 minutes, until thickened. Season to taste and then set aside the filling until you are ready to assemble the pie.

WATERCRESS SAUCE

Prep time: 15 minutes
Cooking time: 20 minutes

INGREDIENTS

2 tablespoons olive oil or
rapeseed oil

2 medium onions, peeled and
chopped finely

1 teaspoon freshly squeezed
lemon juice

150g watercress, chopped finely

600ml soya milk or other plant milk

4 teaspoons tamari

Salt and freshly ground
black pepper

Hot water, as needed

METHOD

In a saucepan, heat the oil on medium heat, add the onion and sweat until
softened. Next stir in the lemon juice and cook for a minute or so.

Add the watercress and soya milk and simmer on low heat for 10 minutes
(be careful not to boil the milk). Remove from the heat and blend in the pan
with a hand-held blender.

Return to the heat, add the tamari and season well with salt and black
pepper. Bring to serving temperature, adding a little hot water if needed to
bring the sauce to your preferred pouring consistency.

ASSEMBLING THE PIE

Spoon the filling into a medium casserole dish. Top with the potato and
spread evenly over the filling. Either smooth the surface of the mashed
potatoes with the back of a spoon or rake over lightly with a fork (I prefer
the texture of the latter).

Bake in the oven for 20–25 minutes or until brown and crusty on top.

Serve with steamed green leafy vegetables, garden peas and the
watercress sauce.

'FORFAR BRIDIES'

Makes 4 pies
Prep time: Pastry:
10 minutes (+ resting for
30 minutes) / Filling:
15–20 minutes
Cooking time:
55–60 minutes

A bridie is an individual Scottish meat pie originating in the town of Forfar, north of Dundee. It is usually made with savoury shortcrust pastry and filled with seasoned crushed steak, butter and beef suet. It looks a little like a Cornish pasty but contains no potato. In this plant-based version I use mushroom, onion and aduki beans, with a wholemeal pastry pie crust. The result is a tasty treat!

INGREDIENTS FOR THE FILLING

1 tablespoon olive oil or rapeseed oil

½ tablespoon sesame oil

1 medium onion, peeled and chopped finely

2 cloves of garlic, peeled and crushed

150g chestnut or button mushrooms, chopped finely

2 tablespoons vegan vermouth (or alternative, see p. 21)

1 x 400g tin aduki beans, drained (240g net weight), rinsed

100g frozen garden peas

1 teaspoon yeast extract or Marmite mixed with 3 tablespoons hot water

2 teaspoons Biona worcestershire sauce (you could also use tamari mixed with a little mixed spice and a pinch of muscovado sugar and omit the teaspoon of tamari below)

2 teaspoons mushroom ketchup (you could also use brown sauce)

1 teaspoon tamari

1 teaspoon dried oregano or 3 teaspoons fresh oregano, chopped finely

5g shiitake or other dried mushrooms rehydrated with 50ml cold water and chopped finely, liquid retained

PASTRY

You will need 1 quantity (300g) of Savoury Shortcrust Pastry (p. 40), kept cool until needed. You can also use shop-bought vegan shortcrust pastry, if you prefer.

METHOD

Preheat the oven to 200°C. Cover a medium baking tray with baking parchment.

In a medium saucepan, heat both oils (olive/rapeseed, and sesame) on medium heat, add the onion and sweat until softened. Add the garlic and cook for a minute, stirring, followed by the mushrooms. Cook for 3–4 minutes, stirring often.

Increase the heat to medium-high, add the vermouth and cook until the liquid has evaporated (about 2–3 minutes).

Reduce the heat to medium and add the aduki beans, peas, yeast extract, worcestershire sauce, mushroom ketchup, tamari, oregano and rehydrated mushrooms (including any remaining liquid) and cook, uncovered, for 5–6 minutes.

Stir in the chickpea flour mixture and cook for a further 3–4 minutes, stirring often, until the filling has thickened (this will ensure the mixture isn't too wet for the pastry). Season with salt and black pepper to taste.

1 tablespoon chickpea (gram) flour mixed with 2 tablespoons cold water

Salt and freshly ground black pepper

Soya milk or other plant milk for glazing

ASSEMBLE AND COOK THE PIES

Remove the pastry from the fridge and divide it into four pieces. On a well-floured surface, roll out each piece of pastry into a square (about 14cm x 14cm) and place each onto the baking tray.

Spoon equal amounts of the filling along the right diagonal side of each square of pastry, forming a triangular mound and leaving 1cm or so of pastry around the edge (this is to try to ensure the filling does not leak). Bring the left-hand piece of the square over the right to form a pasty shape and then seal and crimp the edges with your forefinger and thumb.

Brush the pies with a little soya milk. Place in the preheated oven and cook for 15 minutes to crisp up the pastry. Reduce the heat to 180°C and continue cooking for a further 10–15 minutes until the pies are brown on top.

Serve with a green salad or steamed green leafy vegetables and Tomato Ketchup (p. 41) or other sauce. The bridies also go well with chutney on the side.

A word about . . . aduki beans

Aduki (or azuki or adzuki) beans are a small reddish brown bean with a white speck. They are high in protein and fibre and are also a good source of iron, magnesium, potassium, zinc and folic acid.

To prepare aduki beans, soak them in cold water overnight. Discard the soaking water and rinse the beans thoroughly. Choose a saucepan with a lid, and add the beans. Cover with fresh water twice the volume of the beans. Bring to the boil without the lid on, boil for 10 minutes, then reduce to a simmer, adding the lid at this point, and simmer for around 60–75 minutes or until tender. Drain any excess liquid away. The beans can now either be used or cooled and refrigerated for use the following day.

'HAGGIS'

Serves 6
Prep time: 15–20 minutes
Cooking time: 100 minutes

Haggis is usually served with 'neeps and tatties' for an elaborate Burns Night Supper on 25th January to celebrate the birth of Scotland's national poet, Robert Burns.

This vegan version uses oatmeal, chickpeas, sweet chestnuts and traditional seasoning.

INGREDIENTS

150g quinoa, rinsed thoroughly in cold water (you can also use the same quantity of cooked lentils if you prefer)

450ml vegan stock

50g medium oatmeal

1 x 400g tin chickpeas (240g net weight)

90g roasted sweet chestnuts (vacuum-packed and already peeled, e.g. Merchant Gourmet)

50g hazelnuts, chopped finely

2 tablespoons olive oil or rapeseed oil

4 small onions, peeled and chopped finely

2 medium carrots (about 150g), scrubbed or peeled and grated

3–4 large cloves of garlic, peeled and crushed

100g button mushrooms or chestnut mushrooms, sliced finely

1 teaspoon dried thyme or 3 teaspoons fresh thyme, leaves picked and chopped finely

1 teaspoon dried rosemary or 3 teaspoons fresh rosemary, leaves picked and chopped finely

6 fresh sage leaves, chopped finely

1 teaspoon ground allspice

½ teaspoon ground nutmeg

2 tablespoons tamari

2 teaspoons freshly squeezed lemon juice

Salt and freshly ground black pepper

METHOD

Preheat the oven to 200°C. Line a 23cm rectangular loaf tin with baking parchment.

In a large saucepan with a lid, place the quinoa and the stock, bring to the boil, then reduce the heat and simmer, uncovered, until the quinoa has absorbed most of the liquid and the germ separates from the seed (a small 'tail' will appear) – about 20 minutes. Take off the heat, replace the lid on the pan and cook for another 5 minutes or so. Fluff up with a fork, then stir in the oatmeal and set aside.

While the quinoa is cooking, drain the chickpeas, reserving the bean water/aquafaba to use in another recipe (see Scotch Mist, p. 192), then place in a large bowl and mash, leaving some small pieces. Crumble in the chestnuts and hazelnuts and set aside.

In a large frying pan or heavy-based pan heat the oil on medium heat, add the chopped onion and carrot, and sweat until softened. Next, add the crushed garlic and cook for a minute, stirring. Now add the sliced mushrooms and cook for a further 5 minutes or until softened. Stir in the thyme, rosemary, sage, allspice, nutmeg, tamari and lemon juice.

To the bowl containing the chickpea mixture, add the quinoa and the contents of the frying pan and stir well together. Season to taste with salt and a good few twists of black pepper (traditional haggis recipes are peppery!). Spoon into the loaf tin, press down evenly and smooth the top with a palette knife.

Cover the top with tin foil and cook in the oven for 20 minutes, before removing the foil and returning to the oven for a further 15–20 minutes or until the top is brown and crisped.

'HERRINGS' IN OATMEAL

Serves 2–4
Prep time: 15–20 minutes
Cooking time:
45–50 minutes

In the past Scottish produce, and particularly herrings, was smoked, usually over peat and seaweed, in order to preserve it. Kippers are probably the best-known smoked herring. In my vegan alternative, smoked tofu with celeriac and oatmeal makes for a delightfully savoury plant-based meal! Do try to use smoked tofu, as it adds a whole other dimension to this dish.

INGREDIENTS

1 medium celeriac, peeled and cut into cubes

1 tablespoon sesame oil

1 medium onion, peeled and chopped finely

1 celery stick, trimmed and chopped finely

1 medium eating apple, such as Braeburn, unpeeled, cored and chopped finely

100g smoked tofu (such as Taifun), cut into small cubes

2 teaspoons mushroom ketchup or Biona worcestershire sauce (if you have neither, you could use tamari mixed with a little mixed spice and a pinch of muscovado sugar and use 1 further teaspoon of tamari – see below)

3 teaspoons tamari

90ml apple juice

1 tablespoon vegan Calvados (optional)

2–3 tablespoons water

Salt and freshly ground black pepper

INGREDIENTS FOR THE OATMEAL TOPPING

170g medium or pinhead oatmeal

30g plain wholemeal flour

Salt and freshly ground black pepper

50ml olive oil or rapeseed oil

10g sesame seeds

10g pumpkin seeds

METHOD

Preheat the oven to 180°C.

Steam the celeriac for 6–7 minutes. Set aside. Meanwhile, in a medium frying pan or saucepan with a lid, heat the oil and sweat the onion and celery until softened.

Add the chopped apple and steamed celeriac and cook for 2–3 minutes. Next stir in the tofu, mushroom ketchup, tamari, apple juice and Calvados, if using, and cook on a low-medium heat, covered, for 10–12 minutes. Add a little water to loosen up the mixture if it is looking too dry. Season to taste.

While the celeriac mixture is cooking, make the oatmeal topping. Place the oatmeal and flour in a medium bowl and mix together with a pinch of salt and black pepper. Add the oil and rub it into the flour with your fingertips until the mixture resembles breadcrumbs. Stir in the sesame seeds and pumpkin seeds.

Spoon the celeriac mixture into a medium ovenproof casserole dish, even out the top and finish with a layer of oatmeal topping. Press down firmly, then bake in the preheated oven for 20–25 minutes or until the topping is nicely browned.

Serve with steamed dark-green leafy vegetables drizzled with rapeseed oil.

KALE AND LENTILS

Serves 4
Prep time: 15–20 minutes
Cooking time: 40 minutes

Amazingly tasty and nutritious, and so easy to prepare, I bring you Kale and Lentils – a little jazzed up with tomatoes and herbs!

INGREDIENTS

1 tablespoon olive oil or rapeseed oil

1 onion, peeled and chopped roughly

3 cloves of garlic, peeled and crushed

3 fresh tomatoes, chopped roughly

250g dried red lentils, rinsed thoroughly

1 litre vegan stock

1 teaspoon dried thyme or 3 teaspoons fresh thyme, leaves picked and chopped finely

¼ teaspoon ground mace

3 bay leaves

½ teaspoon freshly squeezed lemon juice

200g kale (thick stems removed), chopped roughly

Salt and freshly ground black pepper

METHOD

In a large, heavy-based pan heat the oil on a medium heat, add the onion and sweat until softened. Add the garlic and cook for a minute, stirring. Then add the tomatoes and cook for 2–3 minutes.

Next, mix in the lentils, stock, thyme, mace, bay leaves and lemon juice. Bring to the boil, turn down the heat and simmer, uncovered, for 10 minutes.

Add in the kale and simmer for 20 minutes, stirring regularly. It will be quite thick. Season well with salt and black pepper, and remove the bay leaves.

Serve with a sprinkle of sesame seeds and with cooked brown rice or quinoa.

LEEK AND MUSHROOM FLAN

Serves 6

Flan base
Prep time: 10 minutes
Cooking time: 15 minutes

Filling
Prep time: 10 minutes
Cooking time:
45–50 minutes

This super savoury flan uses oats and nuts in a crumbly crust rather than pastry (although you could use shortcrust pastry instead if you like). Leeks and mushrooms are a classic combination in Scottish cookery and, together with some fragrant herbs, they impart wonderful flavours to the tofu filling.

This dish can be eaten hot for supper or cold for lunch or turned into a dinner party main course.

INGREDIENTS FOR THE BASE

200g rolled oats

25g cashews, chopped roughly

25g almonds, chopped roughly

25g pumpkin seeds, chopped roughly

5g dried shiitake mushrooms, ground to a powder

½ teaspoon dried oregano or 1½ teaspoons fresh oregano, chopped finely

½ teaspoon vegan stock powder

¼ teaspoon salt and 3–4 twists of freshly ground black pepper

5 tablespoons olive oil or rapeseed oil

Cold water as needed

INGREDIENTS FOR THE FILLING

2 medium leeks, trimmed and sliced into 2cm (or so) rounds (about 250g prepped)

1 tablespoon olive oil or rapeseed oil

1 large onion, peeled and chopped finely

(continued overleaf)

METHOD

Preheat the oven to 180°C. Line a 22cm fluted tart case with baking parchment.

To make the base, place all of the ingredients in a food processor, except the oil and cold water, and pulse half a dozen times. Add the oil and pulse until the mixture resembles coarse breadcrumbs. Add 1–2 tablespoons of water and pulse again.

Scoop the mixture, which will be fairly loose at this point, into the tart case and with the back of a spoon press down firmly and evenly into the base and up the sides a little.

Partially bake in the preheated oven for 15 minutes, then remove and set aside.

While the base is baking, start on the filling. First, steam the leeks for 5 minutes in a steamer. Set aside.

In a medium frying pan, heat the oil on medium heat, add the onion and sweat until softened. Add a splash of hot water if the onions start to stick. Add the garlic and cook for a minute, stirring. Then add the mushrooms and cook for 3–4 minutes. Stir in the steamed leeks and the mustard. Add the vermouth or stock and simmer until the liquid has evaporated (about 3 minutes). Remove from the heat and set aside.

2 large cloves of garlic, peeled and crushed

100g chestnut mushrooms or button mushrooms, chopped roughly

2 teaspoons English mustard

75ml vegan vermouth (or alternative, see p. 21), or vegan stock

250g medium firm tofu, drained

A small bunch of parsley, chopped finely

2 teaspoons dried thyme, or 6 teaspoons fresh thyme, leaves picked and chopped finely

1 teaspoon za'atar (optional, but adds a taste kick)

1 teaspoon freshly squeezed lemon juice

1 tablespoon nutritional yeast flakes

Salt and freshly ground black pepper

75ml soya cream or other vegan cream

In a large mixing bowl, mash the tofu with a fork. Add the parsley, thyme, za'atar (if using), the lemon juice and yeast flakes, stir well, and then season to taste.

Combine the leek and mushroom mixture with the tofu. Stir in the soya cream and adjust the seasoning. Spoon the filling into the pre-baked flan base, even it out and bake in the oven for 30 minutes or until browned and crisped on top.

This dish can be eaten cold for lunch with a green salad, pea shoots and kale sprinkles, or turned into a dinner party main course served with dark-green leafy vegetables and fresh bread.

LENTIL AND BEETROOT BURGERS

Makes 8 burgers
Prep time: 30 minutes
(+ sprouting time for the
lentils) + 30 minutes
chilling time
Cooking time:
15–20 minutes

I first tried a beetroot and sprouted lentil burger at a vegan festival and loved the flavours so much I went home and worked out a recipe of my own. It is worth the effort of sprouting the lentils both for the great texture they provide and for your digestive health. If time is scarce, pre-sprouted lentils can also be found in supermarkets. You can make the burgers a day ahead if you like and refrigerate them overnight before cooking.

INGREDIENTS

100g buckwheat

200ml cold water

½ tablespoon olive oil or
rapeseed oil

1 medium onion, peeled and
chopped finely

3 cloves of garlic, peeled and
crushed

3 medium cooked beetroot (about
200g), peeled (see Preparing Fresh
Beetroot, p. 99, or if using shop-
bought, without vinegar and
well-drained)

100g sprouted green or brown lentils

25g walnuts, chopped roughly

25g hulled hemp seeds

A small bunch of fresh dill, chopped
finely to make 2 tablespoons

1 teaspoon dried marjoram

½ teaspoon smoked paprika

1 teaspoon maple syrup (optional)

1 flax seed egg (1 tablespoon ground
flax seeds mixed with 3 tablespoons
cold water and set aside for a few
minutes to thicken)

50g medium oatmeal + extra if
needed

Salt and freshly ground black pepper

Brown rice flour or chickpea (gram)
flour for flouring and coating

Olive oil or rapeseed oil for shallow
frying

METHOD

Rinse the buckwheat well and add it to a medium saucepan with a lid. Pour over the water, bring to the boil, reduce the heat and then simmer, covered, for around 10–12 minutes or until all the liquid has been absorbed. In the final minutes of cooking, stir to avoid the buckwheat sticking to the pan. Set aside to cool a little.

While the buckwheat is cooking, in a medium frying pan heat the oil on medium heat, add the onion and sweat until softened. Add the garlic and cook for a minute, stirring. Set aside.

Into a large bowl, grate the beetroot. Add the sprouted lentils, walnuts and the hemp seeds and mix together. Then stir in the cooked onion and garlic mixture. Add the cooked buckwheat, dill, marjoram, smoked paprika, maple syrup (if using) and the flax seed egg. Stir in the oatmeal and combine thoroughly to form a sticky mixture. If your mixture is a little wet, add a little more oatmeal. Then season with salt and black pepper to taste.

Preheat the oven to 180°C. Line a baking tray with baking parchment or foil.

Sprinkle rice or gram flour generously on a side plate. With well-floured hands, form burgers of your preferred size. I make mine with a scoop of mix that fits into the palm of my hand and pat it firmly into a fairly thick burger shape. Roll the burgers in the flour and set aside on a second, lightly floured plate until you have used up the mixture. Then place in the fridge for half an hour to firm up. If you are making the burgers well ahead (up to 24 hours), cover with a plate and refrigerate until you want to cook them.

In a large frying pan, heat the oil on medium-high heat, add the burgers and fry them on each side for about 3–4 minutes or until crisped on top. Then transfer to the baking tray and bake in the preheated oven for 10–12 minutes, turning once.

Serve with garden peas, pea shoots and sourdough bread or in a Morning Roll (p. 117) with a leafy green side salad.

A word about . . . sprouting lentils

In a sprouting jar with perforations in the lid place 100g of lentils rinsed well (I find green or brown lentils sprout best). Fill the jar with cold water, close the lid and leave for twelve hours. Rinse away the water, re-fill the jar with fresh cold water and rinse away the water again. Turn the jar upside down on a saucer to drain and place in a warm room.

Rinse the lentils in cold water at intervals two to three times a day for three or four days until sprouts appear. There will be little tails to begin with; what you want are long tails or full sprouts.

Rinse once more, then place in the fridge. Use within a day if making Beetroot and Sprouted Lentil Burgers, or keep refrigerated for several days (being sure to rinse the sprouts each day to avoid any unhealthy bacteria growing) and sprinkle over salads, soups or stews.

MAC AND CAULIFLOWER 'CHEESE'

Serves 4
Prep time: 10 minutes
Cooking time: 15 minutes

The classic mac 'n' cheese, a great favourite in Scotland, is given a healthy plant-based makeover here, and includes nutritional yeast flakes, which add a distinct cheesy flavour. The dish provides a triple boost of calcium from the almonds, the fortified soya milk and the cauliflower, and extra protein from the wholewheat pasta!

INGREDIENTS

1 quantity of vegan cheese sauce (recipe follows)

200g wholewheat macaroni (e.g. Biona; or use a wholewheat pasta such as Gomitini which looks like macaroni; you could also use a gluten-free pasta)

250g cauliflower, cut into small, bite-sized florets

INGREDIENTS FOR THE VEGAN CHEESE SAUCE

100g cashews, roughly chopped

50g almonds, roughly chopped

200ml cold water

1 teaspoon freshly squeezed lemon juice

250ml unsweetened soya milk or other plant milk

4 tablespoons nutritional yeast flakes

2 tablespoons hulled hemp seeds

1 teaspoon garlic granules

1 teaspoon onion powder

1 teaspoon English mustard

½ teaspoon vegan stock powder

A pinch of chilli powder

A good pinch of ground turmeric

Salt and freshly ground black pepper

METHOD

Preheat the oven to 180°C.

Begin by making the cheese sauce. In a large saucepan place the cashews and almonds, cover with the cold water and stir in the lemon juice. Bring to the boil, then reduce the heat and simmer for 10 minutes or until the liquid has been absorbed.

While the nuts are softening, fill a steamer saucepan with cold water, bring to the boil and add the macaroni to the saucepan and the cauliflower to the steamer. Steam the cauliflower for 5 minutes, then remove from the heat, drain and set aside; continue cooking the macaroni until it is tender. Drain the macaroni and return to the saucepan with the cauliflower.

To a blender jug add the softened nuts and the remaining cheese sauce ingredients, except the salt and pepper, and blend until smooth. Season to taste.

To assemble the dish stir the cheese sauce into the cooked cauliflower and macaroni. Bring to a serving temperature, stirring continuously for a couple of minutes, then serve with cooked garden peas and pumpkin seeds, or with dark-green leafy vegetables of your choice.

'MINCE' AND GRAVY

Serves 4
Prep time: 15 minutes
Cooking time: 40 minutes

Mince is a Scottish staple. My plant-based alternative uses protein-rich tempeh instead of mince, smothered in sumptuous onion gravy. This is healthy comfort food and a great way to start exploring tempeh (see A word about . . . tempeh, p. 69).

INGREDIENTS FOR THE MINCE

1 tablespoon olive oil or rapeseed oil

1 large onion, peeled and chopped finely

2 tablespoons vegan brandy (or alternative, see p. 21)

1 tablespoon tamari

1 x 250g block of fresh tempeh (or frozen and defrosted according to packet instructions)

250ml vegan stock

Salt and freshly ground black pepper

150g frozen peas

INGREDIENTS FOR THE GRAVY

1 tablespoon olive oil or rapeseed oil

2 onions, peeled and chopped finely

2 large cloves of garlic, peeled and crushed

2 tablespoons vegan brandy (or alternative, see p. 21)

500ml vegan stock

1 teaspoon yeast extract/Marmite mixed with 2 tablespoons hot water

½ teaspoon dried thyme, or 1½ teaspoons fresh thyme, leaves picked and chopped finely

1 tablespoon vegan sherry

1 teaspoon apple cider vinegar

1 tablespoon flour mixed to a paste with 2 tablespoons cold water

Salt and freshly ground black pepper

METHOD

In a large frying pan, heat the oil on medium heat, add the onion and sweat until softened. Next, add the brandy and cook for a minute or two (to release the juices from the pan). Then stir in the tamari. Crumble in the tempeh, add the stock and cook for around 5 minutes, stirring continuously. Season well with salt and black pepper.

To make the gravy, heat the oil on medium heat in a large saucepan, add the onions and sweat until softened. Add the garlic and cook for a minute, stirring. Then add the brandy and cook for 2–3 minutes to allow the liquid to evaporate. Add the stock, yeast extract/Marmite mixture, thyme, sherry and apple cider vinegar and simmer for 8–10 minutes, stirring now and then. Then add the flour mixture and stir continuously until the gravy starts to thicken. Season to taste.

TO ASSEMBLE THE DISH

Tip the tempeh 'mince' and the peas into your gravy, simmer for 4–5 minutes and then check seasoning and adjust, if needed. Serve with Skirlie (p. 165) or Champit Tatties (p. 160) and dark-green leafy vegetables.

MUSHROOM, BORLOTTI BEAN AND ALE PIE

Serves 3–4
Prep time: 15 minutes
Cooking time:
50–55 minutes

This is a flavoursome dish to offer to non-vegans (as well as vegans, of course!), as it is rich and savoury. The beans provide protein, the mushrooms contain vitamin D as well as protein, and the walnuts are rich in omega-3 fats. You can also serve this as a casserole with cooked brown rice, quinoa or amaranth, if you don't want to use a rich puff pastry topping. For a variation, change up the peas to carrots, parsnips or squash.

INGREDIENTS

1 tablespoon olive oil or rapeseed oil

1 medium onion, peeled and sliced finely

2 large cloves of garlic, peeled and crushed

150g chestnut or button mushrooms, chopped roughly

5g dried shiitake mushrooms soaked in 4 tablespoons hot water, then chopped or snipped with scissors roughly

1 x 400g tin borlotti beans, drained (240g net weight)

50g walnuts, chopped roughly

75ml vegan stock

125ml vegan ale (e.g. Glebe Farm Beer Night Mission is both vegan and gluten-free, as is Daas Ambre; bottled Fursty Ferret and London Pride are vegan)

125g frozen peas

2 teaspoons Biona worcestershire sauce (or tamari mixed with a little mixed spice and a pinch of muscovado sugar)

1 teaspoon dried thyme, or 3 teaspoons fresh thyme, leaves picked and chopped finely

1 teaspoon cornflour mixed with 1 tablespoon cold water

Salt and freshly ground black pepper

250g ready-made vegan puff pastry, such as Jus-Rol (defrosted if frozen)

METHOD

Preheat the oven to 200°C.

In a heavy-based pan, heat the oil on medium heat, add the onions and sweat until softened. Add the garlic and cook for a minute, stirring. Then add the fresh mushrooms and cook for a further 4–5 minutes.

Next, add the rehydrated dried mushrooms and soaking liquid, borlotti beans, walnuts, stock, ale, peas, worcestershire sauce, thyme and cornflour mixture. Bring to the boil and simmer for 8–10 minutes until most of the liquid has been absorbed and the sauce has thickened. Season well with salt and black pepper.

Spoon the mixture into a round 18–20cm ovenproof casserole dish and cool to room temperature.

Keep the puff pastry chilled but workable until needed. Then, on a floured surface, gently roll out the pastry to just larger than the casserole dish. Using the rolling pin, lift and lay the pastry over the dish, crimp the edges, cut off any excess pastry with a knife, and cut a couple of slits in the pastry topping to release steam while cooking. Place the pie in the middle of the oven and cook for 25–30 minutes or until the top has puffed up and turned golden brown.

Alternatively, to avoid a soggy pastry crust, cut out the pastry to the right size to fit your casserole dish and then cook it separately on a baking sheet for the same amount of time as the filling. Once cooked, place the pastry over the top of the pie.

Serve with steamed dark-green leafy vegetables.

SAGE AND ONION 'SAUSAGES'

Makes 8 sausages
Prep time: 15–20 minutes
Cooking time: 40 minutes

A good home-made vegan sausage recipe is useful for quick evening meals as well as a 'full Scottish' breakfast on the weekend. The main ingredient is butter beans, which can take plenty of flavour, so season well and use fresh thyme and sage if possible. The sausages can be made ahead and refrigerated overnight.

INGREDIENTS

2 tablespoons olive oil or rapeseed oil

2 medium onions or 1 large onion, peeled and chopped finely

3 large cloves of garlic, peeled and crushed

2 tablespoons vegan vermouth (or alternative, see p. 21)

12 fresh sage leaves, chopped finely

1 teaspoon dried thyme, or 3 teaspoons fresh thyme, leaves picked and chopped finely

1½ teaspoons onion powder

1 teaspoon garlic powder

2 teaspoons Biona worcestershire sauce (or tamari mixed with a little mixed spice and a pinch of muscovado sugar)

½ fresh lemon

Water, as needed

Salt and freshly ground black pepper

1 x 400g tin butter beans, drained (240g net weight), rinsed in cold water

100g medium oatmeal

25g dried apple rings, chopped finely, then mixed with 3 tablespoons hot water

Brown rice flour or chickpea (gram) flour for coating

Rapeseed oil or olive oil for shallow frying

METHOD

Preheat the oven to 180°C. Line a medium baking tray with baking parchment.

In a medium frying pan, heat the oil on a medium heat, add the onion and sweat until softened. Add the garlic and cook for a minute, stirring. Next, pour in the vermouth and cook off the liquid for a minute or two. Add the chopped sage, thyme, onion powder, garlic powder and the worcestershire sauce and cook for 2–3 minutes, adding a good squeeze of lemon juice (to taste) and a splash of water if needed to keep the mixture moving in the pan (but not sloshing about). Season well with salt and black pepper, then remove from the heat and set aside.

In a large mixing bowl, mash the butter beans with a potato masher or fork and then stir in the oatmeal. Add the apple, then transfer over the onion and sage mixture and stir together well. Season further, if needed.

Sprinkle some flour onto a side plate and also flour a dinner plate. With floured hands, take a handful of the mixture, roll it into a sausage shape and coat the sausage in flour from the side plate before placing it on the dinner plate. Repeat until all of the mixture is used.

Either chill the sausages, covered, until ready to cook or heat a large frying pan on medium heat, with enough oil to just cover the bottom. Gently fry the sausages for 3–4 minutes, turning frequently to ensure they brown and crisp up evenly.

Place them on the prepared baking tray and bake in the oven for 20 minutes, turning once halfway through the cooking time.

Serve with leafy green vegetables and boiled new potatoes or in a roll with Tomato Ketchup (p. 41) and a green side salad.

SANDY'S BEANS

Serves 6–8
Prep time: 25 minutes
(+ overnight soaking, if
using dried beans)
Cooking time: 1 hour and
45 minutes (mostly
unattended)

This is my husband Sandy's recipe and he always uses dried beans from scratch; there is an option, too, for using tinned beans, if you prefer! These haricot beans are slow-cooked which makes them totally moreish!

INGREDIENTS

300g dried haricot beans + 150ml vegan stock (or 3 x 400g tins haricot beans, drained (net weight 240g per tin))

2 medium carrots (about 150g), scrubbed or peeled and sliced roughly

3 beef (or large) tomatoes (about 600g)

100ml olive oil or rapeseed oil

2 large onions, peeled and chopped finely

1 celery stick, trimmed and chopped finely

5 cloves of garlic, peeled and crushed

2 tablespoons tomato purée

1½ tablespoons fresh oregano, chopped finely

A small bunch of parsley, chopped finely to make 2 tablespoons

5 cloves

2 bay leaves

¼ teaspoon chilli powder (optional)

¾ teaspoon salt

Freshly ground black pepper

METHOD

Place the beans and carrots in a large pan with a lid, cover them with water to about 3cm higher than the beans and simmer, with the lid on, at a low heat for about 45 minutes or until softened. Drain in a colander retaining the liquid in a bowl and return the beans to the pan.

If using tinned beans, drain the beans and add them to a bowl. Steam the carrots until soft and add them to the beans. Set aside.

In a large pan, blanch the tomatoes (i.e. cover with boiling water for a couple of minutes), drain the water and, when cool enough to handle, peel the tomatoes and mash them with a potato masher (yes, this is right) and discard the skins.

In a large frying pan, heat the oil and cook the onion and celery for about 5–10 minutes. Stir in the garlic and cook for a couple of minutes. Then add the pulped tomatoes, tomato purée, oregano, parsley, cloves, bay leaves, chilli powder, if using, salt, and several twists of black pepper to taste. Mix well and simmer at a low heat, covered, for about 25–30 minutes, stirring from time to time.

Next, to the large pan of prepared beans and carrots, add the sauce from the frying pan and 150ml of the retained bean liquid (or the 150ml vegetable stock, if using tinned beans) and simmer at a low heat for another 30 minutes.

Serve with Sage and Onion 'Sausages' (see p. 146) and steamed broccoli or kale. The beans are also a scrumptious filling for baked potatoes or baked sweet potatoes and make for luxury beans on toast!

If there are beans left over, cool what you don't use, and divide into containers and freeze for up to three months. Just remove the beans from the freezer several hours before you want to reheat and serve them.

SHEPHERDESS PIE

Serves 4–6
Prep time: 20 minutes
Cooking time: 75 minutes

Shepherdess Pie is one of my all-time favourite meals. The 'mince' is made from protein-packed lentils, mushrooms and walnuts which also provide great taste and texture.

INGREDIENTS FOR THE FILLING

200g split red or brown lentils, rinsed well

1 tablespoon olive oil or rapeseed oil

1 large onion, peeled and chopped finely

4 medium carrots (about 300g), trimmed, scrubbed or peeled, and chopped finely

1 celery stick, trimmed and chopped finely

2 cloves of garlic, peeled and chopped finely

100g chestnut or button mushrooms, chopped finely

100g walnuts, chopped roughly

2 tablespoons sesame seeds

350ml vegan stock

2 teaspoons yeast extract/Marmite + 2 tablespoons tomato purée mixed with 4 tablespoons hot water

2 teaspoons Biona worcestershire sauce

1 teaspoon dried oregano, or 3 teaspoons fresh oregano, chopped finely

Salt and freshly ground black pepper

INGREDIENTS FOR THE TOPPING

800g floury potatoes, peeled and quartered

1 tablespoon olive oil

100ml soya milk

Salt and freshly ground pepper

METHOD

Preheat the oven to 180°C.

Place the lentils in a medium saucepan with a lid and cover with cold water to around 2cm above. Bring to the boil and cook for 5 minutes on a rolling boil, then reduce the heat and simmer, partially covered, for around 15 minutes or until the lentils have softened, stirring from time to time. Add a little more water if required to keep the mixture moving.

While the lentils are cooking, prepare the topping. Bring the potatoes to the boil, then reduce the heat and simmer, partially covered, for 12–15 minutes. Drain, then add the oil and milk, mash and season to taste.

To continue making the filling, heat the oil in a heavy-based pan, add the onions, carrots and celery, and sweat until softened, stirring regularly; this may take 15–20 minutes. Then add the garlic and cook for a minute, stirring. Next stir in the mushrooms and mix well.

Now, add the walnuts, sesame seeds, stock, yeast extract/Marmite and tomato purée mixture, worcestershire sauce and oregano. Cook for around 10–12 minutes, uncovered, stirring regularly, until the liquid is absorbed, then mix in the cooked lentils and season to taste with salt and black pepper.

Spoon the lentil mince mixture into a 20cm round ovenproof casserole dish. Cover evenly with the potato mash (you can either smooth over the top with a palette knife or make little ridges using a fork – I prefer the latter) and cook in the preheated oven for 25 minutes or until the potato topping is golden brown and crisping on top and the pie is heated through.

Serve with Tomato Ketchup (p. 41) or your favourite branded sauce and steamed dark-green leafy vegetables.

SMOKED TOFU CASSEROLE

Serves 4
Prep time: 10–15 minutes
Cooking time: 45 minutes
(mostly unattended)

This is a nourishing dish, ideal for anyone new to plant-based cooking who is looking for an easy and healthy supper recipe. And an appealing way to introduce tofu to the uninitiated!

INGREDIENTS

1 onion, peeled and sliced finely

1 head of fennel, trimmed and sliced finely

1 bunch of asparagus, trimmed and cut into 3–4cm pieces

1 x 500ml bottle of vegan cider (e.g. Dunkerton's Black Fox Cider)

750ml vegan stock

1 teaspoon dried oregano or 3 tablespoons fresh oregano, chopped finely

200g smoked tofu (such as Taifun), cut into small cubes

200g frozen peas

Salt and freshly ground black pepper

METHOD

Place the onion, fennel, asparagus, cider, stock and oregano in a large casserole dish or saucepan with a lid. Bring to the boil, reduce the heat, then simmer with the lid on for 30 minutes.

Add the tofu pieces and cook for a further 10 minutes, uncovered, before adding the peas, then bring back up to heat (the frozen peas will lower the temperature of the liquid) and cook for a further 4–5 minutes.

Season to taste with salt and black pepper, ladle into warm bowls and serve with seeded bread.

SPRING VEGETABLE BAKE

Serves: 6–8
Prep time: 25–30 minutes
Cooking time:
60–65 minutes

This plant-based bake is made with protein-rich quinoa and Scottish spring vegetables. It is super filling and a family favourite. I love to serve it smothered with Cashew Cream Cheese (p. 29).

INGREDIENTS

200g quinoa, rinsed thoroughly in cold water

600ml vegan stock

3 medium carrots (about 225g), trimmed, scrubbed or peeled and sliced finely into half-moons

150g broccoli florets, chopped into bite-size pieces

1 tablespoon olive oil or rapeseed oil

1 medium onion, peeled and chopped finely

1 medium leek, trimmed and sliced finely

3 large cloves of garlic, peeled and crushed

3 tablespoons vegan vermouth (or alternative, see p. 21)

2 teaspoons dried oregano, or 6 teaspoons fresh oregano, chopped finely

A small bunch of parsley, chopped finely

1 teaspoon English mustard

½ teaspoon freshly squeezed lemon juice

2 tablespoons hulled hemp seeds or sunflower seeds

2 tablespoons nutritional yeast flakes

1 flax seed egg (1 tablespoon ground flax seed mixed with 3 tablespoons cold water and set aside for 5 minutes to thicken)

2 tablespoons chickpea (gram) flour + more if needed

Salt and freshly ground black pepper

METHOD

Preheat the oven to 200°C. Line a 23cm x 13cm deep-sided tin with baking parchment.

Place the quinoa and the stock in a large saucepan with a lid, bring to the boil, then reduce the heat and simmer, uncovered, until the quinoa has absorbed most of the liquid and the germ separates from the seed (a small 'tail' will appear) – about 20 minutes. Take off the heat, add the lid to the pan and finish cooking for another 5 minutes or so. Fluff up with a fork and set aside.

While the quinoa is cooking, steam the carrots and broccoli for about 6 minutes. Set aside.

In a large frying pan, heat the oil on medium heat, add the onion and leeks and sweat until softened. Next, add the garlic and cook for a minute, stirring. Add the vermouth and keep stirring until the liquid has evaporated (about 2–3 minutes). Add the steamed carrot and broccoli, the oregano, parsley, mustard and lemon juice and cook for a minute or two.

Add the cooked quinoa to the mixture in the frying pan, stir in the hemp seeds or sunflower seeds, yeast flakes, flax seed egg and chickpea flour and combine thoroughly. Add a little more flour if the mixture seems too wet. Then season well with salt and black pepper.

Scoop into the prepared baking tin and smooth the top with a palette knife. Bake in the preheated oven for 40–45 minutes or until the top is nicely brown and crisped up.

Remove from the oven, cut into thick slices and serve with cashew cream cheese and a large green salad. You could also fill burger buns with slices of the bake and top with the cream cheese, lettuce and slices of tomato.

'STOVIES'

Serves 4
Prep time: 25 minutes
Cooking time: 60 minutes

Stovies have long been a staple in the Scottish diet and traditionally are made using potatoes and onions fried in dripping and meat jelly; they also often contain leftovers of minced beef. This more healthy, plant-based version uses potatoes and onions together with olive oil, lentils and a little fresh rosemary and makes a very satisfying (and, according to my tasters, an apparently authentic) dish!

INGREDIENTS

3 tablespoons olive oil

500g onions, peeled and sliced finely

1kg potatoes, peeled and sliced finely

A large sprig of fresh rosemary, leaves picked and chopped finely

½ teaspoon ground nutmeg

300ml concentrated vegan stock

Freshly ground black pepper

115g dried red lentils, rinsed in cold water

Salt as needed

METHOD

In a large heavy-based pan with a lid, gently heat the oil, add the onions and sweat slowly over a low heat for about 20 minutes.

Add the potatoes, rosemary, nutmeg and stock and a couple of twists of black pepper, place a lid on the pan and cook gently until the potatoes are soft, about 40 minutes, only stirring them if they look like sticking.

In a medium pan, place the lentils, cover with cold water to around 2cm above, bring to the boil, reduce the heat and simmer, uncovered, for 20 minutes or until all the water has been absorbed. Stir towards the end of the cooking time and add a little more water if necessary. The lentils should just yield when squished between finger and thumb and not be mushy.

Add the cooked lentils to the potato mixture, season to taste and heat to serving temperature.

This goes really well with leafy green vegetables sprinkled with sesame seeds. Stovies make a tasty accompaniment to Black Bean and Mushroom 'Black Pudding' (p. 48).

THREE NUT 'MEAT' LOAF

Serves 4–6
Prep time: 20–25 minutes
Cooking time:
55–60 minutes

Meatloaf, generally made from minced Scotch beef, is a popular Scottish dish and has different regional variations. My plant-based take on it uses three types of nuts which *can* be grown in Scotland: hazelnuts, walnuts and sweet chestnuts! I can vouch for the fact that walnuts grow in Scotland, as I have seen a walnut tree along the banks of the River Tweed near the Borders town of Melrose.

This nut loaf also contains an optional 'secret' Scottish ingredient: whisky! And it includes dried mace, which is often used in old Scottish recipes, but you can use nutmeg instead, if you have it more readily to hand.

INGREDIENTS

100g hazelnuts, ground finely

100g walnuts, ground finely

90g roasted sweet chestnuts (these are generally already peeled and vacuum packed, e.g. Merchant Gourmet), chopped finely

100g vegan wholemeal breadcrumbs

1½ tablespoons olive oil or rapeseed oil

1 large onion, peeled and chopped finely

1 medium carrot, trimmed, scrubbed or peeled, and grated

2 tablespoons peaty malt whisky

225ml vegan stock mixed with 1 teaspoon mushroom ketchup and 1 teaspoon Biona worcestershire sauce (if you have neither, you can use 2 teaspoons of tamari mixed with a little mixed spice and a pinch of muscovado sugar)

1 teaspoon dried oregano, or 3 teaspoons fresh oregano, chopped finely

1 teaspoon dried thyme, or 3 teaspoons fresh thyme, leaves picked and chopped finely

½ teaspoon ground mace or ground nutmeg

Salt and freshly ground black pepper

METHOD

Heat the oven to 180°C. Line a 23cm bread tin with baking parchment.

Mix together the hazelnuts, walnuts, sweet chestnuts and breadcrumbs in a medium bowl, then set aside.

In a medium pan, heat the oil on a medium heat, add the onion and carrot and sweat until softened – about 10–15 minutes. Add the whisky and cook for a minute or two to allow the alcohol to evaporate. Then add the stock, oregano, thyme and mace or nutmeg, bring to the boil, reduce to a simmer and cook, stirring occasionally, for 4–5 minutes.

Add the contents of the frying pan to the bowl containing the nuts and breadcrumbs and mix until well combined. Then season well with salt and black pepper.

Spoon into the baking tin and smooth the surface. Cover with foil to prevent the top from burning while cooking and bake in the preheated oven for 20 minutes. Remove the foil at this stage and bake for a further 20–25 minutes or until the top is brown and nicely crisped.

Serve with Skirlie (p. 165) and steamed dark-green leafy vegetables.

Any leftovers can be cooled, covered and chilled, then reheated the next day in the oven at 180°C for 15–20 minutes (covered with foil).

VEGETABLE
ACCOMPANIMENTS

BAKED CARROTS AND SWEDE

Serves 4
Prep time: 10 minutes
Cooking time:
50 minutes
(mostly unattended)

This is my preferred way of cooking root vegetables, as it preserves their wonderful flavour. You can follow the 'par-boil and bake' method with potatoes, parsnips and celeriac as well. If you do not have time to bake the veg, steam them instead; they will still be sweet and tender.

INGREDIENTS

6 medium carrots (about 450g), trimmed, scrubbed or peeled, and chopped into roughly 4cm pieces

¼ large swede, peeled and chopped into roughly 4cm pieces

Salt and freshly ground black pepper

METHOD

Preheat the oven to 180°C.

Place the carrots and swede in a large ovenproof pan. Cover with cold water and bring to the boil. Boil hard, uncovered, for 5 minutes, then remove from the heat and drain away the water.

Add the lid, then place the pan in the oven (i.e. without water) and bake for 45 minutes. Serve hot seasoned with salt and black pepper.

CHAMPIT TATTIES

Serves 4
Prep time: 10 minutes
Cooking time:
15–20 minutes

Tatties, or potatoes, are a traditional staple of the Scottish diet, first introduced to Scotland in the mid-eighteenth century. Potatoes are not only versatile, they are also a high-quality protein and a good source of vitamins B6 and C, as well as potassium and manganese. Champit Tatties – aka mashed potatoes – are also easy and quick to make!

INGREDIENTS

800g floury potatoes (such as King Edward or Maris Piper), peeled and cut into even-sized quarters

1 tablespoon olive oil or rapeseed oil

100ml soya milk or other plant milk

Salt and freshly ground black pepper

METHOD

Place the potatoes in a medium saucepan with a lid and cover with cold water to around 3cm above. Bring to the boil, then reduce the heat and simmer, partially covered, for around 12–15 minutes until tender but not falling apart. Drain off the water (you can use the lid to do this carefully), then add the oil and soya milk, and mash with a potato masher until completely smooth. Season with salt and black pepper.

COLCANNON

Serves 2–4
Prep time: 15 minutes
Cooking time:
25–30 minutes

Colcannon is famous Scottish fare. It brings together two of the country's most humble ingredients: cabbage and potatoes. Colcannon is the Highland name for this dish; it is also called Rumbledethumps in the Scottish Borders (where butter is used in the recipe) and Kailkenny in Aberdeenshire (where cream is used instead of butter). My plant-based version is made using vegan cream and olive oil, and it is simply delicious!

INGREDIENTS

900g floury potatoes (such as King Edward or Maris Piper), peeled and chopped roughly

150ml soya cream, oat cream or other plant-based cream

½ cabbage trimmed and shredded (about 400g prepped)

50ml olive oil

1 medium onion, peeled and chopped roughly

A small bunch of parsley, chopped finely

1 teaspoon ground nutmeg

Salt and freshly ground black pepper

METHOD

Place the potatoes in a medium pan, cover with water to about 3cm above, bring to the boil and cook until the potatoes have softened but are not breaking apart – about 12–15 minutes. Drain and then mash together with the cream and set aside.

While the potatoes are cooking, steam the shredded cabbage for 5 minutes.

In a large frying pan, heat the oil on a medium heat, add the onion and sweat until softened. Stir in the mashed potato, steamed cabbage, chopped parsley, ground nutmeg and season well with salt and black pepper. Heat through before serving.

Try topping with grated melty vegan cheese and then grilling for a meal in itself!

Leftovers can be cooled, chilled and reheated the next day by frying in a pan with a little oil on a medium heat and stirring well for about 5–6 minutes.

CREAMED LEEKS

Serves 4
Prep time: 10 minutes
Cooking time: 15 minutes

I first had vegan creamed leeks on a red double-decker bus in London which had been converted into a restaurant! When I got home, I wanted to replicate the dish and worked out this recipe. These rich, creamy leeks are a scrumptious accompaniment to vegan pies and nut roasts.

INGREDIENTS

3 tablespoons olive oil or rapeseed oil

3 medium leeks, trimmed and sliced finely (about 375g prepped)

3 cloves of garlic, peeled and crushed

2 tablespoons vegan vermouth (or alternative, see p. 21)

1 teaspoon English mustard

150ml soya cream or oat cream

Salt and freshly ground black pepper

Extra soya milk or oat milk, if needed

METHOD

Gently heat the oil in a medium frying pan, then add the leeks and sweat on a low-to-medium heat until softened.

Add the garlic and cook for a minute, stirring. Then add the vermouth and cook for 2–3 minutes until the liquid has evaporated. Next, stir in the mustard and the cream, season well and heat through gently for a minute or two. If the mixture is a little dry at this point, stir in one tablespoon of soya milk at a time until you have your desired consistency and then bring to serving temperature.

NEEPS AND TATTIES

Serves 6
Prep time: 10 minutes
Cooking time: 20–25 minutes

While 'neeps and tatties' are a classic accompaniment to haggis, they can grace any hot savoury dish and can be eaten on their own as the traditional Orkney Clapshot.

INGREDIENTS

¾ swede, peeled and chopped roughly (750g prepped)

6–8 floury potatoes (such as King Edward or Maris Piper), peeled and chopped roughly (750g prepped)

1 tablespoon olive oil or rapeseed oil

100ml soya cream

1 teaspoon ground nutmeg

Salt and freshly ground black pepper

METHOD

Place the swede and potatoes in a large pan and cover with fresh water. Bring to the boil, reduce the heat and simmer for about 20 minutes. Drain and then add the oil and soya cream and mash. Stir through the nutmeg and salt and black pepper to taste. Serve hot.

If you have any leftovers, cool and then refrigerate them; they will keep for a couple of days. They can be reheated either by steaming or by gently frying with a little oil on a medium heat – a kind of Scottish 'bubble and squeak'!

SKIRLIE

Serves 4
Prep time: 10 minutes
Cooking time: 15 minutes

Skirlie is traditionally made with oatmeal, onions and suet and served with mince or mashed potatoes. While it can be made using vegetable suet, my wholesome plant-based version uses olive oil instead. Skirlie also pairs well with a nut roast.

INGREDIENTS

2 tablespoons olive oil or rapeseed oil

2 medium onions, peeled and chopped fairly finely

1 large leek, trimmed and sliced finely

300ml boiling water

50g medium or pinhead oatmeal

Salt and freshly ground black pepper

A small bunch of parsley, chopped finely

METHOD

Heat the olive oil on a medium heat in a large frying pan with a lid, then add the onion and leek and sweat, covered, for 5 minutes. Stir in the water and continue cooking with the pan covered until the onions and leeks have softened – another 5 minutes.

Add the oatmeal and cook for 4–5 minutes, stirring often, until the liquid has reduced. Season well with salt and black pepper and serve immediately, with chopped parsley scattered on top.

DESSERTS

BAKED OATY DATE APPLES

Serves 4
Prep time: 10 minutes
Cooking time:
30–45 minutes (unattended)

Baked apples are an easy-to-prepare autumn dish for when apples are in abundance in Scotland. It is a good pudding to make if you already have the oven on. These are filled with a spiced dried fruit and nut mixture which complements the tartness of the apples.

INGREDIENTS

4 large cooking apples, cored

4 pitted Medjool dates, chopped finely

1 tablespoon demerara sugar

2 teaspoons maple syrup

1 teaspoon ground cinnamon

½ teaspoon ground nutmeg

3 tablespoons roasted hazelnuts, chopped finely

2 tablespoons rolled oats

3 teaspoons non-hydrogenated vegan butter

2 tablespoons vegan ginger wine (e.g. Stone's, UK)

METHOD

Preheat the oven to 180°C.

To prevent the apples bursting when you cook them, carefully score them with the tip of a sharp knife at the midway point all the way round (without cutting them in half) and then place them in an ovenproof dish.

In a small bowl, mix together the remaining ingredients. Spoon a quarter of the mixture into the core of each apple and press down firmly. Bake in the preheated oven for 30–45 minutes, depending on the size of your apples, or until the fruit is soft when tested with a knife.

Serve with vegan cream or vegan vanilla ice cream. Cool and refrigerate any leftovers and have cold the next day for breakfast with porridge or cereal. I love them with cold rice pudding!

BLACKBERRY, APPLE AND CARDAMOM CRUMBLE

Serves 6
Prep time:
10 minutes (topping) +
15 minutes (fruit)
Cooking time: 35–40
minutes (unattended)

Crumble is a much-loved Scottish pudding and there is good reason for this: it combines seasonal fruits – most often and most familiarly autumn apples – with a Scottish staple – oats. It is a firm favourite in our house.

This recipe is at the luxurious end of crumbles, as the topping includes nuts, seeds and nut butter.

I like using pears and stem ginger for a crumble filling, as well as plums and blackcurrants. Adjust the sweetness to taste, depending on the natural sugars of the fruit. Follow the same method as for this filling (using the ingredients listed below).

INGREDIENTS FOR THE CRUMBLE TOPPING

140g rolled oats

60g quinoa flakes (optional, or you can use more oats)

50g wholemeal plain flour

50g demerara sugar or coconut sugar

A pinch of salt

2 heaped tablespoons pumpkin seeds

2 heaped tablespoons chopped roasted hazelnuts

50g hazelnut butter (or other nut butter)

45ml olive oil

METHOD

Preheat the oven to 190°C.

Begin by preparing the crumble. Place the oats, quinoa flakes (if using), flour, sugar, salt, pumpkin seeds and hazelnuts in a medium mixing bowl and stir together well. Add the nut butter and oil, and rub it into the flour with your fingertips until the mixture resembles very coarse breadcrumbs. Cover with a cloth and set aside until the filling is ready.

INGREDIENTS FOR THE FILLING

3 large Bramley (cooking) apples or about 5 smaller ones

3–4 drops of freshly squeezed lemon juice

150g punnet of blackberries

½ teaspoon ground cardamom

½ teaspoon ground cinnamon

1 tablespoon demerara sugar

2 tablespoons maple syrup

2 tablespoons hot water

INGREDIENTS FOR THE PEAR AND STEM GINGER CRUMBLE

4 large pears, unpeeled, cored and sliced

2 pieces of stem ginger in syrup, chopped finely

3 tablespoons hot water

INGREDIENTS FOR THE PLUM AND BLACKCURRANT CRUMBLE

600g plums, cut in half and stones removed

100g fresh blackcurrants, stalks removed (or frozen blackcurrants)

4 tablespoons vegan port

3 tablespoons hot water

Fill a medium bowl with cold water and a few drops of lemon (this stops the apples from turning brown). Peel, core and cut the apples into thin slices and place them in the bowl. Drain the water away and lay the apple slices in the bottom of a square 20cm ovenproof pie dish.

Cut the blackberries in half and mix them with the apples.

Sprinkle the cardamom, cinnamon, demerara sugar, maple syrup and hot water over the fruit and stir everything together until well mixed. Place in the preheated oven and bake for 20 minutes.

Remove from the oven and turn the temperature down to 175°C. Spoon the crumble mixture over the top of the fruit, ensuring that all of the fruit is covered. Press firmly so the mixture is compact and then smooth the top over with the back of a spoon.

Cook in the oven for around 15 minutes, or until the crumble topping is golden brown and the fruit softened when tested with a knife. If the fruit needs a little more cooking but the top is done, cover with foil and cook for a further 5 minutes or so. Serve with Vanilla Custard (p. 42) or Ice Cream (p. 34).

A word about . . . Scottish fruits

Blackberries (brambles) grow wild in the hedgerows in Scotland and are readily available in season in August and September, which is why they make such a great accompaniment to windfall or autumn cooking apples. Blueberries (also known as blaeberries, bilberries or whortleberries), gooseberries, raspberries, redcurrants and strawberries are also grown in Scotland.

You can use any fruits for a crumble and experiment with a range of combinations: apple and blackcurrant, pear and ginger, plum, or raspberry and strawberry. I've suggested a couple of my favourites.

BLACKCURRANT PARFAIT

Serves 4
Prep time: 10 minutes
(+ freezing time of at least
3 hours)
Cooking time:
15–20 minutes

This is an intensely flavoured and vibrant-looking dessert and one of my summertime favourites. Blackcurrants are rich in vitamin C and contain useful amounts of vitamin A and B vitamins, and important minerals such as copper, calcium, iron, magnesium, manganese, phosphorus and potassium, so this has some health-giving properties as well as being a fruity frozen delight!

INGREDIENTS

220g fresh blackcurrants, stalks removed (or frozen blackcurrants)

75g soft brown sugar

3 tablespoons maple syrup + extra if needed

2 tablespoons cold water (none if using frozen blackcurrants)

150ml soya cream or other vegan cream

TO SERVE

Vegan white chocolate, grated (optional)

METHOD

Place the blackcurrants in a medium saucepan with the sugar, maple syrup and cold water. Bring to the boil, then reduce the heat and cook for 15–20 minutes or until the fruit is thick and 'jammy'. Remove from the heat and set aside to cool a little. Pass the blackcurrants through a sieve over a blender jug, discarding the pulp. Add the cream and blend until fully combined. Taste and add a little more maple syrup if needed.

Scoop into a freezer-proof container with a lid and smooth over the surface with the back of a spoon. Freeze. Remove after 1 hour, then again after 2, stirring well each time, then return to the freezer for at least another hour – 3 hours in total.

Remove from the freezer and thaw until you can use a spoon to scoop out the parfait.

Serve in dessert glasses with vegan white chocolate grated on top, if you like.

BOOZY BAKED PLUMS

Serves 4
Prep time: 5 minutes
Cooking time: 20 minutes

This is such a simple and delicious dish. Plums, almonds and almond liqueur go beautifully together. It is like eating frangipane. Boozy baked plums can be served with Macadamia Whipping Cream (p. 32) for added luxury.

INGREDIENTS

8 large or 12 small plums, cut in half and stones removed, chopped roughly

3 tablespoons maple syrup

3 tablespoons Disaronno (vegan almond liqueur)

1 teaspoon vanilla extract

1 teaspoon almond extract

30g flaked almonds, toasted, to serve

METHOD

Preheat the oven to 190°C.

In a medium ovenproof dish, place the plums cut-side down. In a medium bowl, mix together the maple syrup, liqueur, vanilla extract and almond extract. Spoon this over the plums and stir together gently. Bake in the oven for 20 minutes or until the plums are soft and syrupy.

Serve hot or cold in individual dessert glasses with a dollop of macadamia cream and the flaked almonds. The plums keep in the fridge for several days and also make a luxurious topping for porridge or cereal.

CHOCOLATE AND CHERRY MOUSSE

Serves 4
Prep time: 10 minutes

Chocolate and cherry form a very happy partnership. This thick mousse-like dessert is scrumptious, speedy to make and provides good nutrition from the tofu, raw cacao and cherries. Cherries, after being grown successfully on a small scale in Perthshire and Fife, are set to be Scotland's new soft summer fruit crop.

INGREDIENTS

300g carton silken tofu, gently pressed in a sieve to remove any excess water

20g raw cacao powder (or cocoa powder)

1 teaspoon vanilla extract

2 tablespoons maple syrup, vegan honey or coconut nectar (+ a little extra, if needed)

1 x 160ml tin coconut cream, chilled for 30 minutes in the fridge

75g fresh pitted cherries (or drained cherries from a bottle; check carefully for any stones), chopped finely, plus a few extra for decoration

1 teaspoon vegan Kirsch (optional)

METHOD

Place all of the ingredients in a blender jug and whizz until smooth, stopping and scraping down the mixture from the sides a couple of times if needed. Taste and add a little more sweetener, if liked, and blend again. Spoon the mousse into individual dessert bowls and chill for several hours.

Just before serving, add a couple of cherries for decoration, and, if you like, grate a few squares of good-quality vegan chocolate over the top of each mousse.

CLOOTIE DUMPLING WITH ORANGE AND MARMALADE SAUCE

Serves 6–8
Prep time: 25 minutes
Cooking time: 4 hours
(steaming, mostly
unattended)
Equipment needed: pudding
basin, greaseproof paper,
foil, string

A clootie dumpling is a classic Scottish steamed pudding and a real indulgence.

Traditionally, a clootie (or cloutie) dumpling contained suet and was boiled in a bag ('cloot' or 'clout' being the Scots word for cloth). My modern vegan version is steamed in a pudding basin. The suet is replaced with oil and the pudding is served with a zingy orange and marmalade sauce.

According to Scottish cookery writer Sue Lawrence in her book *Scots Cooking* a genuine clootie dumpling has a skin which is created by sprinkling flour and sugar into the cloth before it is filled with the dumpling mixture and I have adopted this part of the tradition.

INGREDIENTS

60g wholemeal self-raising flour +
extra for sprinkling

50g ground quinoa flour (or 50g
more of wholemeal flour)

125g vegan wholemeal
breadcrumbs

2 teaspoons baking powder

125g raisins

125g sultanas

1 teaspoon ground cinnamon

1 teaspoon ground ginger

1 teaspoon mixed spice

½ teaspoon ground nutmeg

1 medium cooking apple, peeled,
cored and grated

1 medium carrot, scrubbed or
peeled, grated

50ml olive oil or rapeseed oil

50ml unsweetened soya milk

2 tablespoons blackstrap molasses

2 tablespoons maple syrup

2 tablespoons dark muscovado
sugar + extra for sprinkling

METHOD

Lightly grease a 17cm pudding basin and dust the inside with a sprinkling of flour and sugar.

In a large mixing bowl place the two flours, breadcrumbs, baking powder, raisins, sultanas and spices and combine. Next, stir in the grated apple and grated carrot.

Place the oil, soya milk, blackstrap molasses, maple syrup, muscovado sugar and flax seed eggs into a bowl and stir together until well combined. Add the wet to the dry ingredients and mix thoroughly, adding a little soya milk or orange juice, if necessary, to loosen the mixture: the consistency should be thick but not stiff.

Scoop the mixture into the prepared pudding basin. Cut a circle from the greaseproof paper and use it to cover the surface of the pudding, then cover the pudding basin with enough foil to hang over the sides a little. Tie securely with string.

A good tip is to measure double the length of string, plus enough for tying. Double the string and pass it around the top of the bowl, drawing in the greaseproof paper and foil. Thread the loose ends through the loop that will have formed, pull each end out to tighten and then form a double knot.

2 flax seed eggs (1 flax seed egg = 1 tablespoon ground flax seeds mixed with 3 tablespoons cold water)

Soya milk or orange juice to mix, if needed

Place the sealed pudding in a large heat-proof saucepan with a lid and fill with boiling water to about halfway up the sides of the basin (be careful not to overfill). Place the pan on a high heat, bring to a boil, then reduce the heat, cover and simmer gently for at least 4 hours, checking the water level regularly and topping it up if necessary.

Remove from the heat and with oven gloves or a tea towel lift the basin carefully from the saucepan. Remove the string, foil and greaseproof paper, and cover the bowl with an inverted serving plate. Turn upside down to release the pudding onto the plate the right way up. Serve with Orange and Marmalade Sauce (recipe follows).

ORANGE AND MARMALADE SAUCE

Prep time: 10 minutes
Cooking time: 15 minutes

I like to use a thick-cut marmalade in this sauce, which means you have nice thick chunks of orange peel providing extra texture and a little extra bite. If you prefer a smoother sauce, use thin-cut marmalade instead. This makes a tangy, luscious and not-too-sweet sauce for pouring over your fruity pudding.

INGREDIENTS

1 large orange, juiced

5 tablespoons carrot juice or water

2 heaped tablespoons Dundee (or other) thick-cut orange marmalade

1 tablespoon dark muscovado sugar

1 tablespoon blackstrap molasses

2 teaspoons cornflour mixed with 1 tablespoon cold water

100ml soya cream

A splash of hot water

METHOD

Place the orange juice, carrot juice, marmalade, muscovado sugar and blackstrap molasses in a medium saucepan. Bring to a medium heat and stir until the sugar in the marmalade and molasses has dissolved. Stir in the cornflour mixture, turn up the heat until a rolling boil is reached, and stir continuously until the sauce has thickened.

Remove from the heat, set aside for about 5 minutes to cool a little and then stir in the soya cream. Heat to serving temperature (do not allow the sauce to boil once the cream has been added), adding a splash of hot water if necessary to bring the sauce to your preferred pouring consistency.

COMPOTE OF DRIED FRUIT WITH GINGER AND LIME YOGHURT

Serves 4
Prep time: 10 minutes
Cooking time: 20 minutes

When cooked, these dried fruits turn deliciously sticky. The ginger and lime yoghurt adds warmth and a little pizzazz!

INGREDIENTS FOR THE DRIED FRUIT COMPOTE

4 dried figs

8 dried (unsulphured) apricots

8 dried prunes, pitted

8 dried apple rings

2 pieces of stem ginger in syrup, chopped finely

½ teaspoon ground cinnamon

½ teaspoon ground mixed spice

6 allspice berries (tied in a small piece of muslin)

3 tablespoons vegan ginger wine (e.g. Stone's, UK) or orange juice

300ml cold water

2 teaspoons olive oil or rapeseed oil

INGREDIENTS FOR THE GINGER AND LIME YOGHURT

100g plain, unsweetened soya or other vegan yoghurt

Zest of 1 lime + freshly squeezed juice of ½ lime

Juice of a 4cm piece of root ginger (peeled, grated and then hand-squeezed, pulp discarded)

1 teaspoon blackstrap molasses + extra if needed

TO SERVE

Hulled hemp seeds (optional)

METHOD

Place the whole figs, apricots, prunes, apple rings, stem ginger, cinnamon, mixed spice and allspice berries in a medium saucepan. Add the ginger wine or orange juice and the water. Stir in the oil.

Bring to the boil, then turn down the heat and simmer, stirring occasionally, until the fruit has softened but still has some texture and the liquid has turned syrupy – about 20 minutes. Remove from the heat and take out the allspice berries.

While the fruit is cooking, in a small bowl mix together the yoghurt, lime zest and juice, ginger juice and blackstrap molasses, adjusting the sweetness to taste.

To serve, divide the compote between four dessert bowls, spoon over the ginger and lime yoghurt and sprinkle hemp seeds over the top, if using.

Chill any leftovers. The compote, which can be eaten cold, and the yoghurt keep well in the fridge for 2–3 days.

CONTEMPORARY CALEDONIAN CREAM

Serves 4
Prep time:
15 minutes + chilling time

This is my contemporary vegan spin on an old Scottish dessert which is traditionally made with orange marmalade, whipped cream and brandy. F. Marian McNeill includes a recipe for Caledonian Cream in *The Scots Kitchen* (1929) which uses marmalade, brandy, sugar, lemon and dairy cream. My recipe combines vegan cream and vegan cream cheese with fresh orange, lemon and marmalade.

INGREDIENTS

125ml soya pouring cream or other vegan cream

150g plain vegan soya cream cheese (such as Original Creamy Sheese)

2 tablespoons Dundee (or other) orange marmalade

Zest of 1 orange + 1 teaspoon freshly squeezed orange juice

Zest of 1 lemon + 1 teaspoon freshly squeezed lemon juice

2 tablespoons + 1 teaspoon maple syrup

1 tablespoon coconut butter or coconut oil, melted

A splash of vegan brandy or apple juice (optional)

Vegan ginger nuts, to serve (optional)

METHOD

Place all of the ingredients, except the ginger nuts (if using), in a medium bowl and whisk until completely smooth. Chill in the fridge for at least an hour. Spoon into individual dessert glasses and serve with crushed vegan ginger nuts, if you like, to add some crunch.

CRANACHAN

Serves 4
Prep time: 10 minutes
(+ preparing and overnight chilling of the Whipped Coconut Cream, if using)
Cooking time: 7–8 minutes

Cranachan is a quintessential Scottish dessert traditionally made with local heather honey and dairy cream. It was eaten to celebrate the Harvest Festival using seasonal fruit, most likely blackberries (brambles). Most recipes now call for raspberries in cranachan and I have followed that tradition. Instead of heather honey, you can use elderflower syrup (which provides a lovely sweet and floral note), maple syrup or vegan honey.

INGREDIENTS

1 teaspoon non-hydrogenated vegan butter or olive oil

1 teaspoon light brown sugar

60g medium oatmeal

4 teaspoons elderflower syrup or maple syrup or vegan honey

4–6 teaspoons single malt whisky

250g raspberries + extra for serving

1 quantity of Whipped Coconut Cream (p. 33) or Soya Cream (p. 32)

METHOD

In a small frying pan, melt the butter or oil on a medium heat. Add the brown sugar and stir until it dissolves. Next add in the oatmeal and cook for about 2–3 minutes, stirring constantly. Set aside to cool.

In a medium bowl, mix the syrup together with the whisky. Gently stir in the raspberries and set aside.

Add the whipped cream to a large bowl and stir in the toasted oatmeal. Add the raspberry mixture and fold in carefully. Spoon the cranachan into four dessert glasses and chill until required. Serve within an hour or two of making, decorated with extra raspberries.

If you prefer a more layered look, keep the toasted oatmeal, raspberries and cream separate and spoon them into your dessert glasses in alternating layers. This is less traditional but does look pleasing!

FIVE FRUIT SALAD
FLAVOURED WITH ELDERFLOWER

Serves 4
Prep time: 10 minutes

This dessert is a glorious combination of fruits which can be grown in Scotland (these are all in season in September) and provides a range of beneficial vitamins, especially vitamin C. The addition of fragrant elderflower brings the fruit salad together and also helps to preserve the fruit once prepared.

INGREDIENTS

150ml fresh apple juice

1 tablespoon elderflower cordial or 2 teaspoons elderflower syrup

A squeeze of fresh lemon (about ½ teaspoon)

1 tablespoon vegan orange Muscat or a non-alcoholic vegan dessert wine

2 ripe plums, halved, stones removed and each half cut into 4 slices

100g strawberries, hulled and halved

100g blackberries, halved if large

100g blueberries

100g raspberries

METHOD

In a measuring jug, stir together the apple juice, elderflower cordial or syrup, lemon juice and orange Muscat (or non-alcoholic wine), then pour the liquid into a medium serving bowl.

Add the fruit to the bowl and gently mix everything together. Chill until required.

When ready to serve, spoon into individual dessert bowls and top with generous dollops of Ice Cream (p. 34) or Soya Cream (p. 32).

Fruit salad is best eaten the day it is made, although this will keep in the fridge for 2 days, covered by a plate.

RASPBERRY AND ALMOND TRIFLE

Serves 6–8
Prep time: 10 minutes +
cooling time
Cooking time: 25 minutes

Often served at Hogmanay or on Burns Night, a traditional Scottish trifle is known as a 'Tipsy Laird', as it includes a generous 'tot' of whisky. My vegan version uses vegan almond liqueur and plenty of delectable Scottish raspberries.

INGREDIENTS FOR THE ALMOND SPONGE

250g organic wholemeal self-raising flour

140g coconut sugar

275ml unsweetened plain soya milk

1 teaspoon freshly squeezed lemon juice

60ml olive oil or rapeseed oil

2 teaspoons almond extract

INGREDIENTS FOR THE TRIFLE

1 quantity of Chia Jam (p. 31) or shop-bought raspberry jam

6 tablespoons Disaronno (vegan almond liqueur) or orange juice

300g fresh raspberries (400g, if making the jam)

1 quantity of Vanilla Custard (p. 42)

25g flaked almonds to decorate (optional)

TO SERVE

Soya cream or coconut cream

METHOD

Preheat the oven to 180°C. Line a 20cm square deep-sided baking tin with baking parchment.

Sieve the flour into a mixing bowl, then stir in the coconut sugar. In a small jug, mix together the soya milk and lemon juice and set aside to curdle and form vegan buttermilk.

Add the buttermilk and the oil to the flour mixture and stir gently to make the cake batter, before adding in the almond extract.

Pour the batter into the prepared baking tin, tap the tin on a flat surface to settle the batter and bake in the oven for 25 minutes or until a metal skewer inserted into the cake comes out clean.

Once cooked, remove from the oven, leave in the tin for 10 minutes, then turn out onto a wire rack and cool completely before using in the trifle.

ASSEMBLING THE TRIFLE

When the almond sponge has cooled, cut about half of it into three long strips about 3cm wide, slice each strip in half lengthways and sandwich together with a little raspberry jam. Cut the strips into 2cm pieces and place them in the bottom of the trifle bowl. Next, pour the almond liqueur or orange juice over the sponge pieces and allow it to soak into the sponge. Spoon the raspberries on top and press them down gently to create a smooth surface for the custard.

Now make the vanilla custard and pour it over the trifle mixture. Cover the bowl with cling film to stop a skin forming over the custard, cool completely and then chill in the fridge until required.

Just before serving, decorate with the flaked almonds, if using. Serve with vegan cream for extra splendour (see p. 32 or p. 33 for recipes).

Keep the remaining cake in an airtight container and enjoy with a cup of tea!

RICE PUDDING WITH STRAWBERRY AND RHUBARB COMPOTE

Serves 4
Prep time: 15 minutes
Cooking time:
35–45 minutes

Rice pudding might seem a little old-fashioned – Victorian even – but I think it deserves a twenty-first-century revival because it is a comforting, nourishing, rich and creamy vegan dessert. What's not to like?

INGREDIENTS FOR THE STRAWBERRY AND RHUBARB COMPOTE

200g rhubarb, trimmed and chopped roughly

200g strawberries, hulled and cut in half

1 star anise

¼ teaspoon cinnamon

1 teaspoon vanilla extract

1 tablespoon coconut sugar or elderflower syrup

2 tablespoons orange juice or water

INGREDIENTS FOR THE RICE PUDDING

80g pudding (short grain) rice

600ml unsweetened soya milk

1½ tablespoons coconut sugar

1 teaspoon vanilla extract

100ml soya cream or oat cream

35g pistachios

METHOD

First make the compote. Combine all of the ingredients in a medium saucepan. Bring the pan to a low-medium heat and, stirring frequently, cook the rhubarb and strawberries until they are soft, the sugar has completely dissolved and the mixture is syrupy. Remove from the heat and take out the star anise. Set aside until ready to bring back to serving temperature.

To make the rice pudding, in a medium saucepan, mix together the rice, milk, sugar and vanilla extract. On a medium-high heat, bring the mixture to just below the boil, then reduce the heat and simmer for around 30–35 minutes, stirring frequently to avoid a skin forming on the milk. When the rice is soft but not mushy, take it off the heat and stir in the cream and pistachios.

Divide between four heat-proof dessert glasses or bowls and top with the warm compote.

Cool any leftovers and then chill – both the rice and compote will keep in the fridge for 2–3 days and is just as lovely eaten cold.

ROASTED STRAWBERRIES AND PEACHES WITH ORANGE MUSCAT

Serves 4–6
Prep time: 10 minutes
Cooking time: 20 minutes

While fresh strawberries make for a simple summer dessert, these roasted strawberries with peaches make a lovely treat. You could also use nectarines, if you like.

INGREDIENTS

300g fresh strawberries, hulled and cut in half

4 peaches, stones removed and sliced

3 tablespoons vegan orange Muscat

2 teaspoons elderflower syrup or maple syrup

1 teaspoon vanilla extract

Zest of ½ medium orange

METHOD

Preheat the oven to 200°C.

In a medium ovenproof baking dish place the strawberries and peaches.

Next mix together the orange Muscat, elderflower syrup or maple syrup, vanilla extract and orange zest in a small bowl or jug. Pour the mixture over the strawberries and peaches and combine gently.

Roast in the preheated oven for 10 minutes, then remove, stir, and return to the oven to cook for a further 10 minutes.

Serve hot or warm with Soya Cream (p. 32) or vegan Ice Cream (p. 34). Any leftovers can be cooled and kept in the fridge for several days and used as a topping on porridge or cereal.

SCOTCH MIST

Serves 4–6
Prep time: 15 minutes
(+ time to make the cream,
if required)
Cooking time: 60 minutes
+ 60 minutes cooling time
(unattended)

We sometimes see mist and fog in Scotland, especially in the east, and so this meringue-based dessert with raspberries and cream is in honour of a Scottish 'haar'!

Make and enjoy this dessert, although perhaps occasionally, as this a very sugary confection. If you are using home-made whipped coconut cream you will need to start this recipe the day before.

INGREDIENTS FOR THE MERINGUE

100ml aquafaba (ideally from a tin of cooked chickpeas; refrigerate the chickpeas and use in one of the recipes in this book!)

1 teaspoon vanilla extract

100g caster sugar

INGREDIENTS FOR SCOTCH MIST

80g crushed vegan meringue

400g fresh raspberries

1 quantity of Whipped Coconut Cream (p. 33), or 200g shop-bought vegan whipped cream

25g flaked almonds, lightly toasted

METHOD

First make the meringue.

Preheat the oven to 100°C (you want a very low oven temperature). Cover a medium baking sheet with baking parchment and set aside.

Pour the aquafaba into a clean bowl and add the vanilla extract, then whisk with a hand-held electric mixer on high speed until soft peaks form (about 7–8 minutes). Next, gradually add the sugar, a dessert spoon at a time, and continue whisking on high speed until the meringue forms stiff peaks (a further 7–8 minutes).

Scoop little mounds of meringue onto the prepared baking sheet, leaving a gap between each. Bake immediately in the preheated oven for 1 hour (leave the oven door closed during the cooking time or the meringues may collapse).

After an hour, turn off the oven and leave the meringues there to cool for a further hour until you are ready to assemble the dessert (i.e. do not open the oven door until the full two hours are up).

ASSEMBLING THE DISH

Crush a couple of meringues (once cooled) in the bottom of an individual dessert dish, cover with a handful of raspberries and a dollop of cream and sprinkle flaked almonds over the top. Serve straightaway.

You can also leave the meringues whole, if you prefer, and layer up the raspberries and cream on top. The meringues will keep for a week if stored in a container in a cool, dry place.

A word about . . . aquafaba

If you haven't come across the wonders of aquafaba (bean water) yet, you will be amazed! Aquafaba is the leftover liquid from cooked beans and is used as a replacement for egg whites in vegan meringue. The bean water from a tin of chickpeas works especially well as aquafaba, although you can use other canned white beans, such as haricot beans. If using the bean water from freshly cooked beans, you may have to heat it to reduce and thicken it.

Whipping bean water and sugar together produces fluffy white meringue. Really! It's important to use a clean bowl, as any oil will destroy the meringue peaks, and to use an electric hand-held mixer or food processor, as whisking by hand doesn't produce enough oomph!

STICKY TOFFEE, PEAR AND GINGER PUDDING WITH STICKY TOFFEE SAUCE

Serves 6

Mmmm. Sticky. Toffee. Pud. Or 'STP', as it is known in our house. This scrumptious vegan version includes a little healthy fruit and some nutrition in the dates, blackstrap molasses, flax seeds, soya milk and wholemeal flour. But this pudding is really about indulgence and, with its gingery and spiced stickiness, is pretty good!

STICKY TOFFEE PUDDING

Prep time: 15 minutes
Cooking time: 35–40 minutes

INGREDIENTS

150g Medjool dates (about 7 or 8 large ones) or other soft dates, pitted and chopped roughly

175ml unsweetened soya milk

1 teaspoon vanilla extract

100g dark muscovado sugar

1 tablespoon blackstrap molasses

50ml olive oil or rapeseed oil

175g wholemeal self-raising flour

2 teaspoons baking powder

A scant ¼ teaspoon salt

½ teaspoon ground ginger

½ teaspoon ground cinnamon

2 flax seed eggs (1 flax seed egg = 1 tablespoon ground flax seed mixed with 3 tablespoons cold water)

1 small, ripe pear, cored and chopped finely, unpeeled

METHOD

Preheat the oven to 190°C.

Line a 20cm square baking tin with baking parchment.

Place the dates and soya milk in a medium saucepan. On a medium-high heat, bring to just below boiling point, then reduce the heat and simmer, uncovered, for about 4 minutes, stirring continuously, until the dates are soft and can be mashed gently with the back of a spoon. Add the vanilla extract, muscovado sugar and blackstrap molasses and stir until the sugar has dissolved. Remove from the heat and stir in the oil.

In a large mixing bowl, sift in the flour, baking powder and salt. Then mix in the ground ginger and cinnamon.

Add the date mixture and flax seed eggs and stir them into the flour mixture. Gently stir in the chopped pear.

Tip the batter, which will be very thick, into the prepared baking tin using a spatula and spread the mixture evenly. Place in the oven and bake for 25 minutes. Test with a cake skewer, and if it doesn't come out clean bake for a further 5 minutes or so.

STICKY TOFFEE SAUCE

Prep time: 10 minutes
Cooking time: 15 minutes

INGREDIENTS

150g Medjool dates (about 7 or 8 large ones), or other soft dates, pitted and chopped finely

200ml hot water

1 teaspoon vanilla extract

A pinch of salt

½ tablespoon blackstrap molasses

50g non-hydrogenated vegan butter

A splash of hot water, if needed

METHOD

Place the dates, hot water, vanilla extract and salt in a medium saucepan. Bring to the boil, then reduce the heat and simmer gently for about 12 minutes, stirring regularly and mashing with the back of a spoon to break up the dates and produce a fairly thick sauce. Next, add the blackstrap molasses and vegan butter and cook for another minute or two. Remove from the heat and, with care, as the mixture will be hot, blend until smooth.

Return to the pan and heat through, adding a little more water if needed to get the desired consistency.

To serve, cut the pudding into squares and arrange on dessert plates, pour over the sticky toffee sauce and finish with a dollop of Soya Cream (p. 32) or vegan Ice Cream (p. 34).

STRAWBERRY SOUP
WITH POPPY SEED SHORTBREAD

Serves 4

Chilled strawberry soup is a summer evening's dessert delight. The poppy seed shortbread provides a satisfying crunch.

STRAWBERRY SOUP

Prep time: 15 minutes (+ chilling time of 2 hours)

INGREDIENTS

350g strawberries, hulled

100ml fresh apple juice

2 teaspoons vanilla extract

30g creamed coconut mixed to a paste with 3 tablespoons hot water

4 teaspoons maple syrup

1 tablespoon soya yoghurt or coconut yoghurt

METHOD

To make the strawberry soup, place all of the ingredients in a blender jug and whizz until smooth and creamy. Taste and add a little more maple syrup if needed. Pour into a jug and chill in the fridge for at least 2 hours.

When you are ready to serve, pour the strawberry soup into dessert glasses, add a swirl of yoghurt and serve with a couple of pieces of poppy seed shortbread.

POPPY SEED SHORTBREAD

Makes 16 squares
Prep time: 15 minutes (+ chilling time of 10 minutes)
Cooking time: 15–20 minutes

INGREDIENTS

100g non-hydrogenated vegan butter

50g demerara sugar or coconut sugar + extra to sprinkle

50g organic white or wholemeal spelt flour

50g brown rice flour

50g semolina

50g cornflour

½ teaspoon vanilla powder

A pinch of salt

1 tablespoon poppy seeds

Preheat the oven to 190°C and line a 20cm square baking tray with baking parchment. Place the vegan butter and sugar in a medium bowl and mash with a fork until well combined. Add the remaining ingredients and bring together with the fork, then with your hands, to form a sticky dough.

Press the dough firmly into the prepared baking tray and smooth out evenly with the back of a spoon, then chill for 10 minutes to firm it up. Once chilled, bake in the preheated oven for around 15–20 minutes or until cooked all the way through. You want the shortbread to be pale golden brown – not too pale and not too brown!

Remove from the oven, sprinkle with a little demerara sugar and cut into squares while still hot. Allow the shortbread to cool in the tray before transferring to a wire rack.

SUPER CALCIUM CARROT AND ORANGE POSSET

Serves 4–6
Prep time: 20 minutes
Cooking time: 10 minutes

This is one of my favourite desserts. Traditionally, a posset was a drink made from milk curdled with ale or wine. In modern times, it is more like a custard made from cream and sugar, and my posset is similar to this.

I use silken tofu in this recipe. Don't worry about the tofu! Or the carrots, for that matter! The tofu gives a rich, creamy consistency to this dish and the carrots blend beautifully with the orange juice and zest to produce a lovely natural sweetness. The tofu, carrots, orange, figs and almonds all provide a good helping of calcium.

INGREDIENTS

250g carrots, peeled and chopped roughly

Juice, zest and flesh of 1 large orange

1 teaspoon agar agar powder

300g carton silken tofu, gently pressed in a sieve to remove any excess water

50g coconut sugar

1 teaspoon vanilla extract

4 tablespoons plain, unsweetened soya yoghurt or coconut yoghurt

2 dried figs, chopped finely, to serve

1 square of vegan spiced-orange dark chocolate, for grating on top

20g flaked almonds, lightly toasted

METHOD

Steam the carrots until tender – about 6–7 minutes. Rinse in cold water and set aside.

While the carrots are steaming, in a small pan place the orange juice, zest and flesh. Bring to the boil and then mix in the agar agar powder. Cook on a high heat for 1–2 minutes, whisking continuously until the mixture thickens, then remove from the heat and cool slightly, but do not set. If it does set, add a little warm water, return the pan to the heat and whisk again.

Place the carrots and the orange juice mixture in a blender jug and whizz until smooth, adding a little water if needed. Then add the tofu, coconut sugar, vanilla extract and yoghurt and blend until smooth, stopping and scraping down the sides if necessary, making sure everything is thoroughly combined. Taste and adjust for sweetness, then pour into a medium glass serving bowl and chill in the refrigerator for at least an hour.

To serve, scatter pieces of fig, grated shavings of chocolate and a sprinkle of toasted flaked almonds over the posset and spoon into individual serving glasses.

SWEET CHESTNUT AND CHOCOLATE TART

Serves 8–12

Sweet chestnuts and chocolate were made for each other! Combined with coconut cream they make a smooth, silky and delicious ganache. With a no-bake almond and hazelnut base which complements the chocolate filling, this tart is good enough to present at dinner parties (or to just have for your tea!).

Almonds and chestnuts provide calcium, and the nuts provide good fats and protein. Chestnuts are also rich in vitamin C and folate, as well as iron and other minerals, and the accompanying fruit provides vitamin C, so there is some goodness in this otherwise extremely rich dessert!

This dish needs to be prepared well ahead as it has several (easy) stages and a final chilling time of 2 hours.

TART BASE

Prep time: 15 minutes (+ chilling time of 30 minutes + soaking time, if needed)

INGREDIENTS

100g almonds

30g hazelnuts

100g pitted Medjool dates (about 5 large ones), chopped roughly; if the dates are too firm, soak them first in hot water for 15–20 minutes and then drain off the soaking liquid

2 tablespoons cacao or cocoa powder

1 tablespoon almond butter

3 tablespoons olive oil

A pinch of salt

METHOD

Set out a 22cm round pie dish.

Place all of the ingredients in a food processor and pulse about a dozen times, then process until the mixture forms sticky crumbs. Spoon the mixture into the tart base and press firmly and evenly into the bottom of the tin.

Chill for 30 minutes while you prepare the filling.

CHESTNUT AND CHOCOLATE FILLING

Prep time: 10 minutes (+ soaking time, if needed)
Cooking time: 5 minutess

INGREDIENTS

200g good quality vegan dark chocolate (70% cocoa solids)

200g sweet chestnut purée (e.g. Merchant Gourmet)

1 x 160ml tin coconut cream

75g soft, pitted prunes, roughly chopped (if they are a little dry, soak in hot water first for 15–20 minutes, then drain off the soaking liquid)

3 tablespoons maple syrup or vegan honey

1 teaspoon vanilla extract

2 tablespoons coconut butter or coconut oil (at room temperature)

A handful of blueberries and raspberries, to serve

Cacao or cocoa powder, for decorating

METHOD

Melt the chocolate in a heat-proof basin set over a pan of boiling water, making sure the water doesn't touch the bottom of the basin (or use a *bain marie*). Set aside to cool but not to re-solidify.

Add the chestnut purée, coconut cream, prunes, maple syrup or vegan honey, vanilla extract and coconut butter (or oil) to a blender jug and whizz until the ingredients are very well mixed.

Pour in the melted chocolate and blend again until fully incorporated, scraping down the sides a few times with a spatula if needed. Taste, then blend in a little more sweetener, if you like.

To assemble the tart, pour the filling onto the prepared tart base and smooth with a spatula. Chill for at least 2 hours. To serve, cut into slices and top with blueberries and raspberries and a dusting of cacoa or cocoa powder.

FURTHER RESOURCES AND READING

Animal Ethics, Veganism and Environmentalism

Animal Liberation (Bodley Head, 2015) by Peter Singer
Cowspiracy: The Sustainability Secret (documentary, 2014)
    www.cowspiracy.com/
Dominion (documentary, 2018) watch.dominionmovement.com/
Earthlings (documentary, 2005) www.nationearth.com/
Eating Animals (Penguin, 2011) by Jonathan Safran Foer
Forks Over Knives (documentary, 2011) www.forksoverknives.com/
Speciesism: The Movie (documentary, 2013) speciesismthemovie.com/
What the Health (documentary, 2017) www.whatthehealthfilm.com/

Fruit and Vegetable Growing

*The Complete Book of Vegetables, Herbs and Fruit: The Definitive Sourcebook
    for Growing, Harvesting and Cooking* (Kyle Books, Revised Edition, 2016)
    by Matthew Biggs, Jekka McVicar and Bob Flowerdew
Fruit and Vegetables for Scotland (Birlinn, 2nd edition, 2018) by Kenneth Cox
    and Caroline Beaton
*The Vegan Cook & Gardener: Growing, Storing and Cooking Delicious Healthy
    Food All Year Round* (Permanent Publications, 2019) by Piers Warren and
    Ella Bee Glendining

Scottish Cookery (Vegan)

Rainbows and Wellies: The Taigh na Mara Cookbook (Findhorn Press, 1995) by
    Jackie Redding and Tony Weston

Vegan Cookbooks with Useful Nutritional Information

Cooking Vegan: Healthful, Delicious, and Easy (Book Publishing Company,
    2012) by Vesanto Melina and Joseph Forest
*Going Vegan: The Complete Guide to Making a Healthy Transition to a Plant-
    Based Lifestyle* (Fair Winds Press, 2014) by Joni Marie Newman and Gerrie
    Lynn Adams
The Vegan Cookbook (Octopus Publishing Group, 2014) by Tony and Yvonne
    Bishop-Weston

Scottish Cookery (Not Vegan)

The Book of Bere: Orkney's Ancient Grain (Birlinn, 2017) by Liz Ashworth
Broths to Bannocks: Cooking in Scotland 1690 to the Present Day (John Murray, 1990) by Catherine Brown
The Claire Macdonald Cookbook (Bantam Press, 1997) by Claire Macdonald
Scots Cooking: The Best Traditional and Contemporary Scottish Recipes (Headline Book Publishing, 2000) by Sue Lawrence
The Scots Kitchen: Its Traditions and Lore with Old-time Recipes (Mercat Press, 1993); first published in 1929 by Blackie and Son Ltd, by F. Marian McNeill
The Scottish Oats Bible (Birlinn, 2016) by Nichola Fletcher

Vegan Nutrition

Becoming Vegan: Comprehensive Edition. The Complete Reference to Plant-Based Nutrition (Book Publishing Company, 2014) by Brenda Davis and Vesanto Melina
Becoming Vegan: Express Edition (Book Publishing Company, 2013) by Brenda Davis and Vesanto Melina
A Guide to Vegan Nutrition (Vegan Publishers, Danvers MA, 2015) by George Eisman
Vegan for Life (De Capo Press, 2011) by Jack Norris and Virginia Messina

Online Resources

BDA: The Association of UK Dieticians (www.bda.uk.com/)
    See the Food Fact Sheet on plant-based diets and plant-based information sources
The British Nutrition Foundation (www.nutrition.org.uk)
    Provides detailed information about healthy living, including the Basics of Nutrition (www.nutrition.org.uk/healthyliving/basics.html), although it is not vegan-specific
NHS Live Well (www.nhs.uk/Livewell/Vegetarianhealth/Pages/Vegandiets.aspx)
    Provides a guide to healthy eating as a vegan
Nutrition.gov (www.nutrition.gov/smart-nutrition-101/healthy-eating/eating-vegetarian)
    Provides a list of websites covering healthy eating for vegetarians and vegans
Vegan Health (veganhealth.org/)
    Contains nutrient recommendations, tips for new vegans, research articles and information in several different languages
The Vegan Society (www.vegansociety.com)
    Go to the Resources section for advice about nutrition and health
The Vegetarian Resource Group (www.vrg.org/nutrition/)
    Offers detailed advice on vegetarian and vegan nutrition. See especially Vegetarian Journal's Guide to Food Ingredients by Jeanne Yacoubou, an alphabetical listing which indicates whether common food ingredients are vegan, vegetarian or not (www.vrg.org/ingredients/)
Viva! – Vegetarians' International Voice for Animals (www.viva.org.uk/) *Provides a variety of health factsheets*

ACKNOWLEDGEMENTS

It has been such a pleasure to work on this book, devising plant-based recipes and cooking and sharing plates of food with many people. I want to thank friends and family for eating my food and taking an interest in vegan cooking, and all the vegan and vegan-curious recipe testers and tasters – including teenagers and students, trained chefs and home cooks – who have helped shape this book: Frankie Barr, Carolyn Barr, Barbara Bell, Bettina Brenner, Catherine Brown, Kate Chedgzoy, Polly Chedgzoy & all the family, Ian Clayton, Judith Crichton, Delia Da Sousa Correa, Michael Davis, Claire Davison, Claudia Dietrich, Jenna Durdle, Karin Haffert, Erika Jones & the Durham student posse, Gerri Kimber, Ralph Kimber, Jesse Miles (Joni Ahimsa), Tegan Parsons, Irene Paterson, Gordon Robertson (for gifs and small gifts!), Roy Skinner, Kieran Smith, Kat Taxidou, Olga Taxidou, Derrick Turner and Lilyth Yu.

Warm thanks to Jan Berridge, Rachel Demuth, Lydia Downey and Helen Lawrence for the best time training with you at the wonderful Demuths Cookery School (demuths.co.uk).

Many thanks to Caroline Trotter (carolinetrotter.co.uk/) for professional photography advice when it was needed most – and for the supply of cherries!

Special thanks to Claire Hider, vegan nutritional therapist (www.vital-spark-nutrition.co.uk/), for recipe-testing, meringue consultation and for checking the nutritional information.

Thanks to all at Birlinn for their enthusiasm and guidance during the making of this book, especially Andrew, Hugh and Liz. Huge thanks to Debs both for the brilliant attention to detail in the editing and keen interest in the contents. A big bundle of thanks also to Mark Blackadder for the fab interior design and Jim Hutcheson for the exquisite cover. Kindest thanks to Ralph Kimber for his help with the index. It has been a magical experience turning my 'kitchen' prose and pictures into a beautiful book.

Most of all, a long, loud and loving shout-out to Sandy Paterson for your constant support, endless shopping, testing, tasting and washing-up, and for your willingness to try anything and everything that came out of the kitchen at any and all hours of the day and night!

This book is dedicated to the animals and in hope of the vegan world to come.

INDEX